Every Man Sees You Naked

Every Man Sees You Naked

An Insider's Guide to How Men Think

David M. Matthews

Every Man Sees You Naked: An Insider's Guide to How Men Think

Published by Wheatmark®
610 East Delano Street, Suite 104
Tucson, Arizona 85705 U.S.A.
www.wheatmark.com

International Standard Book Number: 978-1-60494-028-2
Library of Congress Control Number: 2007942903

This book is dedicated to my beautiful wife, Carla, for all her love, support, patience, and understanding. Without her, life would have no meaning … and be a lot less fun.

Special Thanks to
Chelsea Bayouth
Julie Di Cataldo
Lisa Fishkind
Jill Gentsch
Angela Lovesmith
Katie Maruhnich
Nancy Perry
Lori Scalise
Amanda Tilk
Sumi Yang Reeves

Extra-special thanks go to my parents, whose fifty years of marriage served as a loving inspiration.

Contents

Introduction

I will make two assumptions right off the bat. One is that you are probably a woman. I say that because men already know how they think and spend very little time analyzing their thoughts. Consequently, a book like this would interest them about as much as *Rolling in the Mud for Dummies* would interest a pig (draw your own conclusions about this analogy). Also, this book falls roughly into the genre of self-help, and men avoid those books like they would avoid a blowout sale at Linens 'n Things. The second assumption I will make is that you are constantly frustrated by the inscrutable way a man thinks and behaves. But I can assure you that you are not alone. Millions of women feel as you do. And if every one of them buys this book, I will be wealthy beyond comprehension. So, thank you in advance for helping me get one step closer to my own private island paradise in the South Pacific.

Before we go any further, however, I think it is appropriate that I introduce myself. My name is David M. Matthews (not to be confused with Dave Matthews and his wonderful band), and I am a *man*. That, along with thousands of hours spent counseling female friends, relatives, coworkers, and random strangers in line at Target, is my credential for writing this exposé. So, if you were looking for a scholarly, deeply technical, psychological profile of the male of the species, you've picked

up the wrong book. Go check out anything written by someone with a *PhD* or *MD* behind their name. They're smart, and
they probably really need the money to pay off their college
loans and malpractice insurance. If, however, you're interested
in finding out how men *really* think, described in layman's
terms by a guy who's willing to expose all men's dirty little secrets, then congratulations—you've come to the right place.

At this point, I need to clarify a couple of things. Throughout this book, I will make sweeping generalizations. This is
necessary in order to make a point. Please do not take issue
with this. A generalization is just that—something that is generally true. Yes, there are exceptions, but truly they are few.
This book represents how *most* men think. Also, I will often
refer to men as *we* and address my female readers as *you*. This
is merely my shorthand, designed to quickly differentiate between men and women and help minimize the potential for ad
nauseam usage of those two particular words.

And one final thing: Please know that when you finally do
confront your boyfriend/husband/father/son with the hideous
truths that you have discovered about them in this book, they
will likely categorically deny everything. Then, in the most
nonchalant voice they can muster, they will inquire as to where
you heard what you just told them. The correct response is—
and this is very important, because I'd like to avoid being ac-
costed by mobs of angry men and live to write a sequel—to say
that you read about it in *Cosmo*. They'll believe that, and I'll be
let off the hook and free to show my face at hockey games.

CHAPTER ONE

How Men Think Is Not Wrong

At the outset, it is extremely important that you understand and acknowledge a simple fact: how men think is *not* wrong. Although our brains may operate differently from your own, they work exactly as they were programmed to, just as yours does. It is easy to think any of the following:

- Men are shallow.
- Men are sex maniacs.
- Men don't know what they want.
- Men are commitment-phobic.
- Men are pigs.
- Men are insensitive.
- Men have no fashion sense.
- Men are slobs.

However, those statements are true only if you use the way women think as a baseline and you assert that the way women think is the one and only correct way to think.

Now before you say, "Yes, that's exactly right—the way women think, feel, and perceive things is superior to the way men think, feel, and perceive things," let me remind you that men thought the same thing about themselves for centuries and kept women in subservient positions because of this belief. Were they correct when they made those assertions for all those years? And if not, why exactly is it that making virtually identical statements about men does not qualify you as a female chauvinist pig?

The bottom line is that men think like men and women think like women, and neither way is right, wrong, or superior to the other. Once we recognize this, we can begin to look at the differences between the two schools of thought and start to understand how we can use that knowledge to further enhance our relationship with the opposite sex.

CHAPTER TWO

Men's Prime Motivators

Okay, you're about to take a journey—a whirlwind roll-ercoaster ride through the male brain. Make sure your harness fits snugly and your pockets are free of sharp objects. This could be a turbulent ride, and frankly, I don't want any casualties. All set? All right, here we go.

Men are motivated primarily by two things—money and sex. What about spiritual belief? It's true that many men do hold it in high esteem—as long as it doesn't interfere with money or sex. Are there men who are exceptions to this rule? Sure. But unless you regularly dine in the Vatican commissary, chances are you won't spend much quality time with many of them. So let's talk about these two male motivators, starting with sex. Why start with sex? Because it's more fun.

First, I'll let you in on perhaps our most shocking dirty little secret. From the time we're very young, we imagine what you look like naked. It's not done consciously; it's like breathing or burping—it just happens. And it doesn't matter how young or old you are or whether you're related to us; if we find you even the tiniest bit attractive, at some point we've had a Technicolor centerfold of you stapled to our synapses. And while you're trying to wrap your minds around that, here's dirty secret number two: once we imagine you naked, it's often only nanoseconds before we're mentally having hot, sweaty sex with you.

I can imagine the horrified looks on your faces; you're hoping and praying that this isn't true. I'm sorry to say that it is. Your husband, your son, your father, your cousin, your uncle, your grandfather, your clergyman, your dentist, even your gynecologist (when he first met you)—they have all undressed you with their eyes. No matter how inappropriate you may think it is, every man you know has a mental image of you au naturel. And even though we don't *know* what you look like underneath your underwear, we know what we *hope* you look like. So while the naked snapshots of you in our imagination may not be accurate, they are flattering. That's at least *some* consolation, isn't it?

Before we continue, a few words of clarification might be in order. It is important to state that, pedophiles aside, we generally aren't having lustful thoughts about prepubescent girls. At that stage, you're asexual to us, like the tooth fairy and Eleanor Roosevelt. Such girls therefore don't stimulate our ribald imaginations. However, as soon as you sprout womanly accoutrement, regardless of your chronological age, our brains automatically signal, "Game on!" Additionally, even if we don't find you currently attractive, that doesn't necessarily stop our creative visualizations. Sometimes our minds imagine how you *used* to look—when you were younger, thinner, curvier, and so on. And of course, when we do this, you're always buck naked. So, if you're elderly and obese, take heart. There's probably some young whippersnapper picturing you in your prime in the altogether.

Probably, at this point, more than a few of you are expecting me to apologize on behalf of my gender for our scandalously outrageous behavior. However, I'm not going to do that. Why? Because there's absolutely nothing to apologize for. Since Adam took a bite from that apple (simultaneously giving a computer firm their corporate logo), men have been hard-wired to think that way. It's part of our programming. We see a woman; we imagine her naked—end of story. Well … actually it's not. Often, the imagery leads to a neuro-circulatory phenomenon clinically referred to as "getting a woody." It's a pleasant enough sensation, but it's damned inconvenient if we're in tight pants and we lack an appropriate cloaking device, because holding our hands in front of our protruding crotch is almost never particularly effective. But I digress. Suffice it to say that the whole process is second nature to half the world, and whether you like it or hate it, it is part of who we are.

Okay, enough about sex. Let's talk about men and money. Because men are inherently goal-oriented, we strive to make as much money as possible by doing the least amount of work. It's as simple as that. It's not that we're lazy. It's that hard work merely for hard work's sake makes no sense to us. And men are nothing if not practical. On the other hand, we'll work ourselves to the bone if, in our opinion, the economic reward merits such effort. And we really don't care if the job is fulfilling our emotional needs as long as it meets our monetary ones. This is because we validate our existence by our accomplishments, not by how much we enjoyed the journey. And what pushes us ever forward, striving for more and more money? The promise that the more money we have, the more appealing we will be to you. And the more appealing we are to you, the more likely you are to sleep with us. So, in the end, even our motivation for money is influenced by our sexual desires. What can I say? We have one-track minds. But, hey, at least we're consistent.

CHAPTER THREE

Understanding "Man-Speak"

When I sat down to write this chapter (yes, men do sit down for some things), I struggled a great deal with how to lead into this seminal topic. I finally decided that getting right to the crux of the matter was the best approach, so that is what I'm going to do. So here goes. The long and the short of it is this: *Men and women speak a different language.* It may look the same when you see it written and sound the same when you hear it spoken, but trust me when I tell you that most conversations between English-speaking men and women are in dire need of an interpreter. I know that sounds like hyperbole, but as I will try to explain, it really isn't.

First and foremost, it is important to understand that men and women value conversation quite differently. Men are goal-oriented and pragmatic and their often blunt, utilitarian usage of language reflects this. They're frequently quiet if they have no specific information they wish to impart or acquire. Women, on the other hand, embrace their communication skills, artfully employing them as an important part of their underlying desire to establish a bond (social, romantic, professional) with the person they are talking to. A good conversation can be uplifting and satisfying for you even if no new information is exchanged or problem resolved. That same interaction we might find tedious and ultimately unfulfilling *because we haven't accomplished anything.* The bottom line: You communicate because you like to. We communicate because we have to.

Okay, so men don't enjoy talking as much as women do. That doesn't mean that when they do talk their speech should be incomprehensible. That's true. But add to that the fact that, along with men being practical in their speech, our thinking process is remarkably simple and straight-forward. And again our use of language reflects this. In other words, *we say precisely what we mean.* This may be confusing to you, because women have been socialized to analyze or "read into" what is said. This is very useful when you're talking with other women, because they are likely doing the same thing. But men are simple creatures. And though, try as you may to impose upon us a complexity to our thoughts and words, the truth is we're just not as deep as you are. So when we say your hair looks nice, it doesn't mean we hated it before, we don't really like it now, or we secretly want to dump you and we're hoping that a seemingly innocuous hair comment will soften the blow of our impending breakup. No, what we mean is "your hair looks nice, that is, attractive, appealing, pleasant to look at." That's it! No underlying meaning. No hidden agenda. I know you may find this hard to believe, but the key to "man-speak" is that what a man says can be taken at face value. The more you try to analyze it and ask yourself "what did he mean by that?" the more you will ultimately be confused—because we said exactly what we meant. Remember, men wrote the dictionary. We defined the words. And we use them quite literally, without subtext or innuendo.

What all this means is that with one important exception, men are remarkably truthful in what they say. Which is why when you ask us if you look fat in a particular pair of pants, our natural inclination is to answer honestly. You asked a straightforward question, so we're answering likewise. And as brutal as you think that might be, that's how our minds work. As such, if we ask *you* how we look in a pair of pants, we expect that you will be honest with us. We're not looking for affirmation. We're seeking a truthful response. Because of that, if you were to respond, "Your ass looks like it could demand its own zip code," we'd likely just shrug and change our pants. We asked, you answered, mission accomplished.

I mentioned there was one exception to men being completely truthful. Before we sleep with you the first time, you can't believe a word we say. Really. Everything that comes out of our mouths is a lie, carefully constructed to help separate you from your undergarments. We'll shamelessly say anything we think you want to hear to accomplish our single-minded goal. We'll love *Riverdance*, hate Pamela Anderson, and be really interested in meeting your Great Aunt Hortense. No fib too outrageous, no deceit too heinous. We'll lie pathologically. But once we've bedded you and the pressure is off, presto, we become Honest Man, keeper of the truth. I know it sounds weird, but it's absolutely true. And you can believe me, 'cause I'm not trying to get you into bed.

Earlier I spoke of our annoying adherence to the dictionary definition of words. This point requires further elaboration. Because men are literalists, they don't understand or appreciate the subtlety of the nuanced subtexts of women's communication. For us, words generally have the same meaning every time they're used regardless of the context. For you, context is everything. Take, for example, the misunderstanding over the use of the word *fine* in the following dialogue.

Jason: "So, how about we just stay in and order pizza tonight?"
Traci: "Fine."
Jason: "Okay, which do want, Domino's or Papa John's?"

Traci: "I can't believe you."

Jason: "What? You want Pizza Hut?"

Traci: "No, I don't want pizza at all. I want to go out and get a real meal. Let's go to that new Greek place."

Jason: "Fine."

Traci: "Now you're mad."

Jason: "I'm not mad. I'm hungry. And I said the Greek was fine."

Traci: "Exactly. So where do you want to go?"

As you can see, this is the male-female equivalent of "Who's on First?" Unfortunately scenarios like this play out in many of our lives with disconcerting frequency. And it is simply the result of men hearing your words and taking them at face value. You can blame him for his apparent insensitivity to your feelings, but he won't have a clue what you're talking about. Not because he doesn't listen, but because he doesn't get the deeper meaning behind your response. To him, when something's "fine," it means you're cool with it. He doesn't realize that to you, "fine" can mean exactly the opposite: You're unhappy with the situation and a satisfactory solution needs to be forthcoming. So now you're annoyed and he doesn't know why. And usually the situation goes downhill from there.

And there are many other words and phrases that have fixed meaning to men and are strictly conditional for women. When a man says yes, he is giving a decisive confirmation. He, therefore, is confused when he discovers his girlfriend's yes is a bit more flexible. He doesn't get that (1) it may have a time limit or expiration attached ("Yes, I like your elephant foot coffee table"); (2) you may actually mean no, but you don't want to hurt his feelings ("Yes, you're the best lover I've ever had"); (3) it may be negatively impacted by stress or a mood shift ("Yes, I'd love to fuck your brains out"), weight gain ("Yes, I'm dying to go to the beach and show off my new bikini"), or bad hair ("Yes, I'd be happy to be in a formal portrait with your whole family whom I've never met"); (4) the right to change your mind and reverse your decision at any time is absolute. Ditto his confusion over the word *no*.

And then there are the different ways we interpret certain phrases. When you tell him "nothing is bothering me," he believes you, although what you may mean is, "I'm really bugged and you should know why." You may simply be looking for a little, reaffirming nudge when you ask, "Should we really be doing this?"—but when he asks the same question it's because he has serious doubts. And generally when he says, "I don't care," it truly means he has no particular preference, not that he has a number of choices in mind that will come to light with the slightest provocation.

Unfortunately, there are too many words and phrases that mean very different things to men and women to elaborate on here. And though I don't have a resolution to this language barrier, if you treat men with the same patience you'd exercise with a foreigner asking directions in broken English, perhaps there is hope for the sexes to co-exist harmoniously. And to be clear, I haven't just encouraged you to tell your man *where to go*. I would never do that ... even though that's one example where even *he* knows not to take you literally.

CHAPTER FOUR

What Men Want

Millions of pages have been written on "what women want." But what about men? Do you know what *we* really want? The answers may surprise you. Generally speaking, we want more of the same. We are, if nothing, creatures of habit, and when we find something or someone we like, we are perfectly contented to stick with it or them henceforth and hereafter. Our attitude is the proverbial, "If it ain't broke, don't fix it." It is that kind of thinking that allows us to go to the same Italian restaurant, week after week, year after year, and always order the same linguini in clam sauce with a side of fried mozzarella. It may give us heartburn every time, but we know we like it, so why check out the scaloppini or the cacciatore and risk being disappointed? Sure we miss out on a wondrous array of culinary treats, but, hey, the clam sauce hasn't let us down yet, so why risk it?

You see, we invented the status quo and are happy as clams (or clam sauce) to give it our heartiest support. As such, we aren't really looking to improve ourselves or initiate huge change that will totally disrupt the comfortable routine we've haphazardly created for ourselves and our loved ones. It's the reason we're generally satisfied with our reflection in the mirror and why we have virtually no interest in self-help or diet books. We're secure in our identity, regardless of our thinning hair and our thickening waistline. Oh sure, we'd like to look like Brad Pitt ('cause then we could get jiggy with Angelina Jolie), but we realize that's never going to happen, so we accept who we are and live with it. Change is just too much work, and work, if it doesn't pay off in dollars and cents or guaranteed nookie, just isn't worth the effort to us. The truth is, for the most part, the only change that men universally desire is … a new sex partner.

I can almost hear your eyebrows raise. Let me explain.

From the time we first learn about sex and start fantasizing about it in both our waking and sleeping states, we imagine ourselves going at it with a cornucopia of beautiful, sexy women. The faces of these hot creatures are ever-changing, but they all share one common attribute—and no, it's not large, succulent hooters. Their one commonality is that each one is distinctly different from all previous paramours, both real and imagined. And it is this constant variety of nubile lasses that fuels our fantasies with the most intensity. To put it in the most vulgar of ways, "the only thing men like more than pussy is … strange pussy." And by *strange*, we do not mean *odd, deformed*, or *endowed with unique, mutant abilities* (although a vagina with super powers would make a hell of a comic book franchise). No, by *strange*, we mean *new to us, heretofore-unexplored territory, an exciting fresh adventure*. Sexually speaking, we're not looking for the perfect woman, we're looking for an endless parade of perfect women. For us, in our fantasies at least, there is no such thing as too much variety.

However, as usual, reality rears its ugly head. Like you, we are socialized into believing that true happiness can be found only in monogamy. And though the very thought of having sex with only one woman now and forever-more is contrary to every fiber of our being, most of us accept this as a necessary, if frustrating, societal convention. And though we'd be thrilled to have the love life of a rock star or NBA player, we understand our lack of musical talent and inability to slam-dunk doom us to a less promiscuous fate.

But sexual variety aside, men are most contented by familiar, repeating patterns of everyday existence. It is, in fact, our ability to embrace the routine of daily life that allows us to go to the same dull, repetitive, often unsatisfying job for thirty or forty years without going crazy, blowing our brains out, or shooting up a McDonald's. So we stand, mystified, by your desire to rearrange the furniture, re-landscape the yard, and replace last year's barely-worn fashions with this year's latest styles. We also don't understand why you constantly seem to want to change your hair color and style. But we're more accepting of this (as long as you don't snip your locks) because it kind of makes you look like a new, slightly different woman. And that makes us hot.

CHAPTER FIVE

When Do Men Need Romance?

When do men need romance? They don't. Ever.

How can that be? Well, think for a minute. What *is* romantic? Thoughtful gifts, candlelit dinners, foot massages, loving words, moonlit strolls on the beach, cuddling in front of a roaring fire, soft music, gentle caresses—all things that make most women feel "warm and fuzzy." And that plus a libation or two usually leads to lovemaking. In other words, romance is a precursor to sex. It sets the stage. It puts you in the mood. But men are almost always in the mood anyway. We don't need our stage set. Hell, we don't even need a stage. And props and costumes are completely unnecessary. So the real and perhaps shocking truth is … romance exists completely for women. And men employ it simply as a strategic initiative in Operation: Get Her Pants Off.

I know what you're thinking. "That's a cynical bunch of crap. Romance has been around for centuries. Poets, painters, sculptors, and playwrights have all been inspired by romantic notions and created works of art that just *reek* of romance. What about them? Certainly they weren't merely bohemian horndogs just aching to get laid." Au contraire. With few exceptions, that's exactly who they were. They wrote love sonnets, painted portraits, and wrote songs about the objects of their affections for only one reason: They knew that if, with a grand, romantic gesture, they could win their beloved's heart, the rest of her anatomy couldn't be far behind.

Why do you think men became artists, poets, singers, and musicians in the first place? Sure, they were moved by their muse. Yes, commerce may have been involved. But primarily, "artistic types" gravitated to their "calling" as a means to meet beautiful babes. (And it's still happening today—think rock stars and rappers.) And why did they use their art for such "nefarious" purposes? Because, for the most part, that was all they had going for them. Remember, throughout history, few artists have been lauded for their social skills, athletic abilities, or striking good looks. Ever seen a picture of Picasso or Salvador Dali? Not exactly model material. And how about Van Gogh? Even with two ears he was no George Clooney. But those guys had talent. And they knew that their success with women was inextricably connected to their artistic accomplishments. So they worked what they had. And the world and their sex lives were better for it.

All this doesn't mean that I think romance is useless. Not at all. It's *very* useful, because it gives guys a tool in our rather limited sexual fulfillment arsenal. And we appreciate all the help we can get. We just recognize romance for what it is: the price of admission, the prerequisites for certification, the dues we have to pay to get our union card. And we do it all for you. Because we want *you*. And you want *it*. And as a result, romance will never die. So invest in Hallmark or 1-800-Flowers. As long as women are wooed by romantic verse and long-stemmed roses and men have penises, those stocks are as close as you can get to a sure thing.

CHAPTER SIX

What Men Like in Bed

Before we delve into this meaty (no pun intended—okay, it was) subject, I must first caution you that the language in this chapter is suited to the subject matter and is therefore both frank and explicit. If you are shocked or annoyed by such language, I suggest you skip this chapter, though the content may prove to be extremely informative. In any case, you've been warned.

One further note: Men are not all the same. Some of the things indicated here may not apply to *every* man. However, the overwhelming majority of men, and therefore most of the men you'll be sexually intimate with, will find these things appealing (though many may be reluctant to admit it).

One of the most important things to remember in dealing with men and sexuality is that we are very visually oriented and thus easily stimulated by what we see. That is why, in general, we are turned on by men's magazines, Internet porn, strippers, and Jessica Rabbit. We view something of a sexual nature and it stimulates us. And that's the way we like it. It's not that our other senses don't enter into our being aroused, they most certainly do, but if you want to kick start an evening of hot sex, think of most men as being sexually from Missouri, the "show me" state.

What We Like about You

Women are beautiful to men precisely because they look like women and not … men—so *viva la différence* (he said in his best Pepé Le Pew accent)! Though that may seem obvious, it still is important that it be mentioned in any discussion of what men like or find attractive. And since, as we just said, *how* women look is significant in our finding them desirable, a brief exploration of this topic seems especially in order here.

Traditionally, the more physically different from men a woman appeared, the better (in men's minds anyway). Men's bodies are basically linear, so we like curvy, shapely women. We're generally hard and muscular (or at least *wish* we were), so you being soft with a little "cush" in the right places is also a plus. Our chests are flat, so your swelling flesh in that region is attractive. We have facial hair, so we appreciate when you don't (the same is true of underarm, leg, and nipple hair). And then there's the matter of the hair on your head. While our hair is generally short, we love, love, love long hair on you. The longer the better. And though you may think a clean, short cut is sexy, if your hair doesn't make it past your shoulders, don't expect to be thought of as beautiful by men. Best you'll get is "cute."

Stimulating You

Though it is perhaps not in keeping with stereotypical male sexual behavior, today's man is often surprisingly turned on by exciting his sexual partner, sometimes experiencing almost as much from giving pleasure as receiving it. And while we love our orgasms, we're really fond of yours as well. So since part of our having a good time is tied to you having a good time, your enthusiasm can really heat things up for us. Conversely, your apathetic indifference to our overtures can be very disheartening (and dis*hardening*), to say the least. I'm not saying that you need to fake orgasm to please us, just don't behave as if you'd rather be trimming your cuticles. And if you think that's asking too much, consider how you'd feel if while you're giving your man your best sloppy, slutty blowjob, he yawns and asks you to hurry things up so he can go pay the gas bill. Even if you weren't tempted to bite what you were sucking, your perception of your mate as a desirable sex partner would be definitely diminished. So remember, if you want your guy to think you're enjoying the party, cut loose and dance. He'll be happy, and you may actually discover you're having a good time.

Stimulating Us

Men are easy. We get a hard-on from a bumpy car ride. So making us come (or *cum*) is no great feat. But doing it with panache, now that's a whole different matter. The following are suggestions of how your man really wants to be treated.

Hand Jobs

They're not just for teenagers anymore. A good hand job is very sexy and is both excellent foreplay and a wonderfully intimate experience when, for whatever reason, your vagina has the night off. As in all things sexual, lubrication is a big plus, so slather some saliva, lotion, or any oil this side of 10W-40 on his pecker and go to town. You'll like the smooth feel, and the squeaky, squishy sound will be a turn-on for you both. And what about technique? Well, I suggest using both hands, unless one of your hands is already occupied stoking your own fires. Don't forget our balls, although gentle inclusion is usually preferred over kneading and slapping. And try verbal encouragement as well. Actual words aren't necessary, just periodic "ooos," "ahhs," moans and groans will be enormously effective at speeding us on our way to "blessed release."

Blow Jobs

Most women are aware of how much men enjoy having their cock licked and sucked (if this is news to you, let me assure you we like it more than we like ESPN—and you *know* how crazy we are for that). Despite this, many of you are merely adequate in your technique. And while you may have had no complaints, that doesn't mean your sucking doesn't … well … suck. Again, our orgasm is less indicative of your fellatio proficiency than our propensity to arbitrarily ejaculate into anything warm, moist, and available. So how can you become a champion fellatrix? (1) Take as much of his penis as possible into your mouth. (2) Whatever part of the shaft remains uncovered, stroke with your hands. (3) Again, lubrication is very important, so feel free to drool all over him. I promise you, he won't mind a bit. (4) Get a rhythm going and stick with it for awhile, starting out slowly then picking up speed as you go. (5) Make periodic eye contact (assuming you're not sucking in the dark). Men find that very sexy, but will almost never ask for it. (6) While most men find it really hot if you swallow their goo, if that's not your thing, dispose of it any way you see fit. Dribbling it out of your mouth and onto your hands, then rubbing it on his chest, or even better, on yours, is sure to silence any complaints he might have over your refusal to ingest his man juice. Doesn't that make you all sticky? Sure, but sex is supposed to be messy. If one or both of you isn't covered in some type of bodily fluid, you're doing something terribly wrong.

Boob Boffing

As you know, guys love tits. So any activity involving this high-ranking hot-spot is going to be especially appealing to men. Therefore, it is no surprise that we are particularly aroused by placing our penis between your breasts and moving back and forth in a fucking motion, enveloped by your soft, womanly flesh. But isn't this maneuver limited to only those select few who are blessed with bountiful boobage? Absolutely not! Almost all women, regardless of breast size can participate. How can that be? I'll explain.

The main thing to remember is that it is the *proximity* of the breast that men find so … titillating. And that includes small to medium boobs as well. The truth is … your hands are almost as important to tit fucking as are your tits. For it is your hands squeezing your breasts together around your partner's pumping penis that create the necessary friction (and *friction* is a penis' best friend). And even if your breasts aren't large enough to encompass a cock, holding whatever titflesh you *do* have against him, while letting your hands caress his penis, makes for a wonderfully erotic experience for your man and his missile. For generously endowed females, it's a rack-rub with a little assist from helping hands. For the more moderately-upholstered, it's a handjob with a titty chaser. Either way, both your hands and your hooters work as a team. Go team!

At the risk of being redundant, I remind you that the other key ingredient of satisfying sex is plentiful lubrication. Boob banging is no exception. Generously douse your chest and/or his manmeat with AstroGlide, KY, or any number of available oils or lotions, because nothing puts a damper on an amorous interlude like chaffed cleavage or a pecker with a friction burn.

One final word about your breasts: Since we are so enamored with them, we are gratified to witness you demonstrating a similar adoration. It's kind of like seeing your loved ones getting along well together. So any holding, caressing, licking, or sucking of your own breasts or nipples will be greeted by a big smile and an appreciative penis. Who says it's hard to figure out what makes a man happy?

Penetration

There is some debate as to whether or not licking, kissing, fondling, fingering, and sucking are considered actual sex. To some, any intimate interpersonal contact constitutes sex. To others, the aforementioned activities are merely foreplay, a precursor to sex, but not sex itself. In other words, close—but no cigar. (Where in the hell did that expression originate?) Regardless of where you stand on this issue, everyone seems to be in agreement on one thing: When the male of the species inserts his penis into a woman's love canal (not to be confused with the notorious New York dumping ground), sex is taking place.

Men begin life by exiting the vagina—a strategic blunder they rectify by spending much of the rest of their lives attempting to jump the turnstile to get back in. It is a constant struggle, but we soldier on with dogged determination. It is a beachhead we have to breach. A mountain we must climb. It is the one constant force that unites all straight men since the beginning of time. It is our quest—and your vagina is our holy grail. (You don't honestly think medieval knights were searching for a jewel-encrusted cup, do you?) And when we're inside you, we have almost no desire to be anywhere else—such is the allure of your moist furrow. "Damn the Crusades! To hell with the Stock Market! Miller Time can wait! I'm 'gettin' some,' so piss off!" (Suddenly I'm British—go figure.)

Due to our near idol-worship of your tropical region, one might think I would spend a great deal of time on this subject. But one would be wrong. You see, despite the fact that all men love to fuck, *how* they like to fuck varies considerably from one man to the next. So I won't presume to tell you I know how best to satisfy your particular man. What I *will* do is tell you about a few things you can do that men generally acknowledge enhance their coital experience.

As I mentioned before, in the sexual arena, your enthusiasm is your greatest asset. Don't be a passive participant. If you're in the missionary position, move around, meet his thrusts, wrap your legs around him, grabs his ass and pull him into you. If you're on top, bounce with abandon, pull his head to your chest, ride him hard. If you're doing it "doggie-style" (everybody's secret favorite), push back when he pushes forward, sway your butt, look back at him, making eye contact. And be verbal. Moans, groans, grunts, gurgles, sighs, heavy breathing, and any *brief* phrases of encouragement or appreciation (phrases like "Oh, yeah," "Like that," "Don't stop," but not, "Thank you I'm having a really nice time," or "Things are turning out splendidly, don't you think?") are all encouraged. And for many men (and a lot of women, as well), "dirty talk" is a real turn-on. So much so, that I'll devote an entire section to that in a few moments.

The plain truth is that if you're exuding a positive vibe, his experience will be much more gratifying, as will your own. And mutually pleasurable fucking is the foundation of a satisfying sex life, which in turn is the cornerstone of a successful male–female romantic relationship. And since, to some extent, that is probably your goal in slogging through these pages, it is a point worth repeating: *If he is happy with your sex life, he is likely to be happy with your relationship.* And conversely, if your love life is less than stellar, he is *less* likely to feel enthusiastic about your relationship, and *more* likely to join a Crusade, start a war, or drink heavily with his buddies. So in the interest of maintaining a good relationship, defeating liver disease, and bringing about world peace, get out there and fuck like you mean it. (I would have said, "Give 'til it hurts," but that just sounds painful.)

The Back Door

Whether they cop to it or not, most men want to try anal sex at least once. Unfortunately, that's one time too many for a lot of women who consider backdoor sex quite literally an "I hear ya knockin', but you can't come in" subject. That is not to say there aren't legions of females who swear by doing it the "Greek" way. There are. But even most of them had to be pressured, encouraged, sweet-talked, or cajoled into engaging in this activity the very first time. So it is fair to say that, for the most part, men are the primary cheerleaders of anal athleticism. ("Hey team, we're in a rut … time to do her in the butt!")

So why are guys drawn to this activity? Good question. And to be completely honest, I'm not sure there's been a definitive scientific study on what possesses a man to want to shove his penis through a passageway that is fundamentally intended for traffic going the other direction, when there's an unoccupied and presumably hospitable vagina only a stone's-throw away. It doesn't seem to make logical sense. But what gets somebody hot is seldom logical. Perhaps the attraction has to do with the "naughtiness" of the act. Or the fact that it gives us a particularly good view of your ass (which we are quite fond of, thank you very much). Or maybe it's the tight fit. Or that we just revel in the sheer, uninhibited, animalistic aspect of it. Whatever the reason, boys like to bang your bare butt. Not as a steady diet, you understand. Your vagina is still our number one, preferred destination. But every now and then, when the planets align in a particular way, we eschew landing in the familiar Sea of Tranquility and instead venture into the mysterious dark side of the moon. What can I say? We're adventurers at heart.

And what advice do I have on this topic? Well, we're so used to having to broach the subject with you, if you really want to heat us up, approach *us* for a change. Say that you want us to do you that way, and watch the color drain from our cheeks … as all our blood makes a mad dash for our nether regions. You'll gain huge brownie points (no pun intended) and you'll go a long way to reaffirm we made a smart choice hooking up with a sexy vixen like you. Just remember, before you dive in (actually, before *he* dives in) liberally lubricate yourself and him (I'm starting to sound like a broken record), go very slowly, and when you're finished insist he does a rub-a-dub-dub on his skin flute before he plays an encore in your other band shell. Also, be mindful that you are much more highly susceptible to HIV transmission when engaging in this practice, so unless you're in a long-term, monogamous relationship, always have him wear a condom when he comes a-knockin' at the back door.

Dirty Talk

While men are very visually oriented, they are also easily influenced, and hence aroused, by the right verbal stimulus. In other words, when you talk dirty, our penises respond. And this is true in both sexual and non-sexual situations. What you say doesn't even have to be overt ("I want you to fuck me"). It can be merely suggestive ("You know, I'm not wearing any panties"). Either is apt to cause a stirring in our loins.

So how can you exploit this knowledge to heighten our sexual experience and turn yourself into the uninhibited slut we all secretly hope you are (when you're with *us* in bed, anyway)? The following information will attempt to clarify the nuances of our dirty-talk predilections. I will, however, issue another language advisory—this list is especially ... how you say ... *raw*.

First, let's talk about anatomical euphemisms, starting with the penis (where all things start, for us). While it answers to many names, our favorite is *cock*. We simply love to hear you call it that. Tell us you want to play with our penis and we'll happily unzip for you. But say you want to play with our cock, and our penis is likely to do the unzipping all by itself. Such is the erotic power of your use of the word *cock*. Why do we prefer *cock* over *dick, prick,* or *pecker*? Because those words are commonly used derisively: "You dick! Why are you being such a prick? I can't believe what a little pecker you are." See? And even when they're not, they don't conjure up the image in our mind of a proudly erect sentry, ever-ready to storm the palace gates on but a moment's notice. No, that image is the strict province of our cock—ready to crow like its namesake should the opportunity arise. And even though the term *cocksucker* is derogatory when someone refers to *us* that way, if a woman is labeled as such, we're scrambling for a pen to write down her cell number.

It strikes me that if I spend as much time on other words and phrases as I did on *cock* (deserving though it may be), this chapter will be too long (which, ironically, isn't usually a problem for the aforementioned male member). I do, however, promise to revisit the colorful world of sexual slang in a later chapter. But for now, let's get back to Talking Dirty 101 and a list of recommended sexual expletives (and their less-effective and thus discouraged brethren). Good: "Fuck me!" Bad: "Fuck you!" Good: "Lick my ass." Bad: "Kiss my ass." Good: "I want to suck on you." Bad: "You suck." As you can see, literal usage of sexual terms are usually very positive, while less literal usage tends to be negative. The following is a more extensive list of words that get us hot.

Hot	Mildly Erotic	Not So Much
Your Body:		
cunt, pussy	slit	vagina
tits	boobs	bosoms
ass	butt	bottom
Our Body:		
balls	nuts	scrotal sack

Hot	Mildly Erotic	Not So Much
Sex Acts:		
fucking	banging	intercourse
suck, lick	blow	orally stimulate
finger (as a verb)	stroke	caress
cum, shoot, squirt	explode	climax
Misc:		
wet, sticky, juicy	moist	humid

These words, of course, are usually combined in phrases for maximum effect (e.g., "Lick my pussy," or "cum on my tits"). Remember, sex talk should be brief and to the point. Anything of a poetic nature is best left to romance novels and is strongly discouraged. (Don't say, "Insinuate your throbbing member into the tropical oasis of my womanhood," unless you want to hear us snicker.) Just think of yourself as an ER doctor with a critically injured patient lying on a gurney in front of you. You need what you need right now, and you don't have time to mince words. ("I want to suck your cock, stat!" Alright, no "stat," but you get what I mean.) And don't be afraid to be a little demanding, as long as what you are asking for is infinitely do-able (e.g., "Lick me there," or "Keep fucking me like that"). But shy away from lascivious orders that might be likely to induce performance anxiety ("Don't cum before me") or questions that are ego-deflating ("Can't you get that fucking thing hard?"). Follow these rules and your guy will feel like he's found the gutter-mouthed girl of his dreams.

As I've said before, sex is a powerful force in men's lives. That's why I've devoted so much space to its discussion. And since it's such a high-ranking priority with us, knowing how we *perceive* all things sexual is imperative to your better understanding of how men think. In a sense, this knowledge gives you the power to have your man practically eating out of your hand (or some other body part). Use it wisely. And while some men may criticize me for "letting the cat out of the bag" on their sexual proclivities and peccadilloes, most will be too busy having a good time with their recently transformed love goddess to even notice.

CHAPTER SEVEN

Mythbuster: Why What You Think You Know about Men Is Wrong

To put it mildly, there are a lot of misconceptions about men. So at this time I feel it is incumbent upon me to "set the record straight" and debunk the most popular and most annoyingly persistent myths and misunderstandings about the male of the species.

1. Men are insensitive.

Actually, nothing could be further from the truth. Men are incredibly sensitive. I offer as proof all the poets, playwrights, painters, and composers down through the ages who have crafted their works with remarkable passion and sensitivity. The overwhelming majority of these inspired and often tortured souls are men. So, yes, men feel deeply. They simply express those feelings in ways very different from the female of the species.

You see, men are socialized to keep their feelings inside. "Big boys don't cry" isn't just something our parents said to us. It's the cement in our psychological foundation. We are told from our earliest recollections to "buck up," "be a man," "walk it off," because to do otherwise and show our pain and/or emotion is socially unacceptable. And there is no greater insult to even the youngest of males than to behave "unmanly." Being branded a "sissy" is social suicide and we do whatever is necessary to avoid even the possibility of being labeled as such. And if that means sublimating our hurt and masking our feelings, so be it.

So we grow up hiding our emotions, never discussing how we feel with any of our contemporaries. Whereas you can spill your guts to your friends and receive guidance, advice, and emotional support, that whole process is off limits to us. We wear our strength and self-sufficiency like a badge of honor, leaving us alone to cope with and resolve whatever issues or internal angst we possess. Thus, our insecurities are masked by arrogance. Our weakness is hidden by bravado. And the only acceptable outlet for all our emotions is athletic competition. Consequently, many of us throw ourselves into sports—playing them, watching them, discussing them, and endlessly analyzing them—for it is one of the only safe venues for us to get excited, yell, scream, cry, and even hug each other without fear of reprisal or being ostracized by our peers. It is our only acceptable emotional release—other than sex (which, of course, isn't a viable option to a prepubescent boy). So next time you see two grown men standing in the stadium bleachers, shirtless, painted blue, and hysterically bumping bellies with each other, you'll understand that this is the male emotional equivalent of a pint of Chunky Monkey and a good cry.

2. When a relationship ends, if my man hurries into the arms of another woman, it's because he really didn't care that much for me.

Because, as we just stated, men don't have the emotional support system in place that women do, we must rely on something else to take away our pain when we are suffering. So after a devastating breakup we realize we must act quickly to shore up our emotional buttresses or risk exposing our soft, emotional underbelly with resulting humiliating repercussions. And instinctively we know that the only way to quell our internal turmoil is to focus our emotions on another appropriate target—a new woman. So we set our sights and move quickly. The more hurt we are, the faster we act. Therefore, it is a reflection of the intensity of the heartbreak how swiftly a man connects with a rebound relationship. Hence, the more in love with you he was, the quicker you'll find him in the arms of another. So if you break up with your guy tonight and tomorrow he's out on the town with a new hottie, you can assuage your hurt feelings with the knowledge that you broke his heart big-time.

3. Men are intimidated by successful women.

No, we're just not particularly attracted to them. Despite what you may think, your success in the workplace (or lack thereof) doesn't really figure in when we're determining who appeals to us. What does matter, other than the way you look and your general attitude, is whether or not you're likely to spend any time or attention on us. Since success usually requires dedication and dedication demands significant time spent focused on your profession, we may perceive you as having little time or energy left for us. So why even pursue you, when there are attractive, available women who aren't so career-obsessed and actually will make time for us? The bottom line is: *We* may be workaholics, but we're not particularly drawn to them.

4. Men like their women thin.

Generally, this is not the case. Although there are men who are particularly attracted to super-thin women, just as there are those drawn to the morbidly obese, most men do not fall into this category. Men like women who look like … well … women. Thin women often have the shape of twelve-year-old boys. So unless you want to appeal to pedophiles or preteen girls, thin isn't necessarily the way you want to go.

What men like are curves. In fact, a recent survey of men indicated that the most feminine attribute (and therefore the most appealing) was a small waist that flared out into wider hips. In other words, we like the classic "hourglass figure." I know this contradicts everything you see in Vogue. But remember, those often-shapeless models are hired by fashion designers (who are rarely heterosexual males) to appeal to women (who *do*, in fact, find thin unbelievably appealing). However, if you want to see what kind of body men like, check out men's magazines, like *Playboy* and *Stuff.* Those women have figures that inspire us to greatness. Or at least arouse us to distraction.

That is not to say you have to look like a Playmate. No, that's just our ideal. As long as there's some shape to your shape we're not that picky. But given the choice (like that's ever going to happen), we'd pick Salma Hayek over Keira Knightley when we're casting the leading lady in our sexual fantasies. Which may lead you to assume—

4. Men only like big boobs.

Not true. Men just like boobs, period. Big ones, small ones, perky ones, pendulous ones. All breasts are welcome. In fact, men are so fond of the female mammary glands that we've devised a plethora of endearing pet names for this anatomical point-of-interest. The following is an alphabetical sampling of these terms (though certainly not a comprehensive list): *apples, baby feeders, balloons, bazookas, b-b's, bee stings, boobies, boobs, bosoms, bounty, bra-stuffers, bust, cans, cantaloupes, casabas, chest, cleavage, coconuts, creamers, cupcakes, cushions, dairy delights, danglers, d-cups, décolletage, dirty pillows, doorknobs, floppers, fun bags, gazongas, (the) girls, hangers, headlights, high beams, honkers, hoohas, hooters, jugs, knockers, lumps, mammaries* (as in "Thanks for the …"), *mams, maracas, melons, milk cans, milkers, mounds, mountains, pillows, Pointer Sisters, pontoons, puppies, rack, snuggle pups, sweater meat, ta-tas* (usually preceded by the modifier *bodacious*), *titties,* (the ever-popular) *tits, twin peaks, whoppers, udders,* and *zeppelins.* And this doesn't even take into account the sub-category of "nipple slang." As you can see, some of us have way too much time on our hands.

I think it is fair to say, therefore, that it is no exaggeration that we're "hot for hooters." And thanks to tight and low-cut fashions, surgery, padding, and underwire, the female rack is now on display more prominently than ever. So on behalf of males everywhere, I say, "Hallelujah!" And we're delighted to see whatever you've got, large, small or in-between. That is not to say that bigger breasts don't catch our eyes. They do—just as bigger diamonds catch yours. But that doesn't mean you don't still find the smaller-caratted solitaire beautiful. And while fake diamonds may repulse you, that is not the case for us and breasts. As long as something looks, feels, and tastes like a tit, we'll love 'em even if they're stuffed with silicon, saline, or soy beans. Men are so egalitarian, don't you know.

5. Men won't respect me if I sleep with them right away/ too quickly/before we really know each other/prior to our wedding night.

Not only are all these statements incorrect, they are built on the false premise that our respecting you or not is somehow tied to our attraction (or lack thereof) to you. The simple truth is this: A man can be enormously attracted to you and not respect you one iota. This concept may be a little difficult for you to swallow (and getting you to swallow things is somewhat of a male preoccupation), as respect is such an important element of women finding men appealing. In fact, most women are totally uninterested in having any kind of physical relationship with a man they don't respect on some level. This, however, is not the case for men. Respect for our female partner is so unimportant that most of us don't even consciously think about it. It simply doesn't matter.

To help you wrap your mind around this concept, let me give you a good example of what I'm talking about. We all remember the enormously popular sitcom *I Love Lucy*. Many of us spent a good portion of our youth laughing hysterically at the exploits of that indefatigable redhead. Lucy was funny, that's for sure. But in my opinion, it is also true that she was one of the most despicable characters in the history of TV. I know that sounds blasphemous, but think about it. Every single week, Lucy would want something and stop at nothing to get it. She'd lie, steal, cheat, and exploit whoever she had to, regardless of if she endangered the health and well-being of her best friend, Ethel, or jeopardized her husband's job or financial future. If Lucy wanted it, screw everybody else. And inevitably, when she would have to face the music (usually a Cha-cha or a Samba) for her devious, self-serving manipulations, rather than admit her mistake or offer apology, she'd cry like a baby who's just pooped her Pampers. Yeah, there's a lot to respect there. And yet, Ricky loved her, unquestionably—the "I" in the title referred to him. Though she was an untrustworthy, selfish sociopath, Ricky dug the hell out of Lucy, so much so, that despite the logistical difficulty of separate beds, they produced drum prodigy, Little Ricky (who is rumored to have played a conga solo of "Babbaloo" in utero). And while this was fiction and Lucy's behavior an extreme example, we bought it, without question. We believed Ricky could continue to be attracted to her week after week, season after season, "'til cancellation do us part." And we accepted this, because, deep down we understood that for men, love could exist and even flourish, when respect was MIA.

Still have doubts? Then perhaps the following conversation will get the point across:

Ted: "Staci's really hot. You're one lucky guy to be dating her."

Paul: "Yeah, but I question her values. I don't think she's a very ethical person."

Ted: "Wow. What a turn-off. So, I take it you're gonna break it off with her."

Paul: "What choice do I have? But since you're so attracted to her, I wouldn't mind if *you* asked her out."

Ted: "No, 'cause then I'd be expected to have sex with her. And it's just too emotionally unsatisfying shoving my penis into a woman I don't respect."

Paul: "I hear you, man."

Now can you really imagine a conversation even remotely similar to that taking place in this time or dimension? Need I say more?

"Okay," you say, "but even if respect isn't an issue, won't sleeping with a guy too soon make him think I'm a slut and ruin any chance for a serious relationship?" The short answer is no, but the explanation for that actually requires substantial elaboration. That, coupled with the fact that I need to fill pages if this is going to be a book and not just a multipart series in *Cosmo*, has caused me to devote an entire chapter of this book to this extremely important topic of men and dating. And it's coming up soon, so read on. (This is about as close as you get to a cliffhanger in this tome.)

One final note: It is important to understand that respecting someone and treating them *with* respect are two very different things. Respect is earned and as we stated, optional. But treating someone respectfully is an absolute necessity for the long-term success of any romantic relationship. So while a man may or may not respect you, if he doesn't *treat* you respectfully, you need to seriously examine why you would want to continue to be involved with him.

6. When a man truly loves you, he won't even think about another woman.

Nonsense. Men think about other women all the time, almost perpetually. But it is absolutely no reflection on your relationship or how hot you are. As previously stated, men automatically picture every woman they see naked, so unless they're living in a monastery, a prison, or a gay bath house (all of which don't bode well for your romantic future), they're thinking of other women every time one walks, runs, or sashays by. This may be disconcerting, but like night following day, it happens whether you or we like it or not. The important thing is that if their heart is truly with you, their wandering mind won't jeopardize their fidelity and thus your relationship.

7. To a guy, there's no such thing as "bad sex."

The truth is, we recognize "bad sex" when we have it, but like lite beer and arena football we accept it when we have no other choice. To be sure, in desperate times, we might even go back for seconds or thirds. But when we realize the quality is lacking, you can be certain we have our eyes on the lookout for *any* other opportunities.

I can almost hear you thinking, "Wait. Men almost always have orgasms during sex, so how can the sex be 'bad?'" The truth is that orgasms are different for us than they are for you. For us, sex and orgasm are almost synonymous. We rarely have one without the other. So having an orgasm doesn't necessarily make our experience, and therefore the sex, "good." It just makes it sex. You see, we kind of take our ejaculations for granted. We expect them. Sort of like a belch after a cold beer. We know it's coming, then it's there and we have a mild sense of relief. But the burp doesn't indicate the quality of the brew. We let one rip whether it's watered-down domestic or the most expensive, imported micro-brew. (I use a lot of beer analogies, because along with sports and sex it is many men's raison d'être.)

The bottom line is this: Just showing up for sex does not make a woman a good sex partner. And since we're likely to climax no matter what, you can't use our "happy ending" as a barometer. But although men *can* differentiate between good and bad sex, we feel that *any* sex is better than *no* sex, so don't expect to hear complaints from us. Just don't read too much into our orgasm. *We* certainly don't.

8. Men will change.

They won't … unless they really want to. And like an alcoholic, drug addict, or compulsive gambler, the desire to alter oneself in any significant way must come from within. So save your breath. Your encouragement, coercion, or nagging will have absolutely no lasting effect. And any *apparent* changes in behavior, dress, or attitude he makes are strictly temporary. They'll last until you stop having regular sex with him or leave the room, whichever comes first. Besides, you knew how he was when you met him. If you were so unhappy with who he was, why did you pursue a relationship in the first place? And if your answer is, "He had potential/He was a fixer-upper," consider how you'd feel if he felt the same way about you. Then again, maybe he did … though this is highly unlikely. Not because you have no flaws, irritating habits, or obvious imperfections. No, it's because this is yet another example of the difference between men and women. The homily says, "Women marry men hoping that they will change—and they never do. But men marry women hoping they won't change—and they always do." Truer words were never spoken (at least in the last ten minutes). And if you strongly disagree, don't blame me, take it out on the homily.

9. Men cheat because something is wrong in their relationship with you.

No, *women* cheat because there is something wrong in their relationship. At least, *traditionally* that was true. A growing trend is for women to cheat for the same reason as their male counterparts. And that reason? Opportunity. *Men* cheat because they have the chance to. Not that every man will succumb to temptation when it presents itself, but even those who do are often perfectly happy in their relationship with their significant other. They just are lacking the discipline and/ or self-control to resist the offer of sex with someone new.

"How can that be?" you ask. "If he loves me and is happy in our relationship, why would he be so easily drawn into the arms of another woman?" The answer is quite simple: For men, monogamy is unnatural. And though we may try to focus all our attention on just one special woman, it is a constant struggle because the idea of "strange pussy" is almost irresistible. And no matter how beautiful, sexy, and good in bed you are, you're still limited to being only you ... not someone new.

As disturbing as this may be, the situation is obviously far from hopeless. Most men control their natural inclination to seek out new, uncharted vaginas by engaging in a rich fantasy life. It is yet another dirty secret of ours that we frequently fantasize we're doing some hot, new chick as we pump in and out of you. It doesn't mean we don't love you or find you incredibly desirable (if we weren't with *you*, we'd probably be fantasizing about screwing *your* brains out while we're nailing someone else). It's simply that we feel the need to change it up every once in awhile. It allows us to remain faithful to you, while satisfying our need for variety. It's a coping mechanism, a mind game we play on ourselves precisely because we *don't* want to cheat on you. And though you may think we are guilty of "mental infidelity," remember thoughts are not crimes. If they were, your thoughts of inflicting a slow, tortuous death on the person who came up with bikini waxing would have landed you in jail a long time ago.

10. Men appreciate women who dress stylishly and are "well-put-together."

Yeah, *gay* men. Straight men, on the other hand, really don't care all that much. We actually prefer you undressed, so anything you wear is just an annoying impediment to our enjoyment of your naked flesh.

That being said, there are some outfits we find sexier than others. We're suckers for skimpy lingerie because it's the next best thing to nothing at all. But mostly we're fans because when you put it on and show it to us, it usually means there's nookie tonight. After that, we like anything that is low-cut, short, or super tight (especially if *you* are). In other words anything that makes you look the least bit slutty, we love. And the sluttier the better. We don't give a damn about Anne Klein, Dolce & Gabanna, Armani, Donna Karan, or Prada. Any outfit that you and your female friends would describe as classy, exquisite, or elegant is likely to leave us completely cold.

I am certainly not saying you should dress for *us*. Dress any way you are most comfortable. Wear whatever you feel exemplifies who you are. Just know that if you ever do want to get the male of the species looking lustfully in your direction, "less is more," and tight tops, short skirts, and "fuck-me" pumps rule. (That is, unless you're already our wife/fiancée/girlfriend, in which case we encourage you to dress in the stylish, sophisticated outfits your mother would call "stunning." Hey, we want you to look slutty for us, not for every Tom, Dick, and Tyler who's sure to be eyeing your assets!)

CHAPTER EIGHT

Why Guys Ask You Out

Dating may well be the most confusing cultural ritual that exists. And although both men and women have a love/hate relationship with dating, it is for very different reasons. You see, because of the complexity of the female of the species, women go on a date for a multitude of reasons: (1) You like a guy and you want to get to know him better; (2) you don't know if you like a guy and you're hoping to get further insight into the matter; (3) you don't like a guy *that way* but he obviously likes you, so it won't kill you to spend a little time with him; (4) you don't really know him, but he piqued your curiosity and you never know, he could be "the one;" (5) your mother/sister/aunt/friend/psychic says he's a great guy, so how bad could he be? (6) you're lonely/bored/broke or just tired of watching *Grey's Anatomy* with your cat and he's paying (the guy, not the cat), so what the hell? (7) you're afraid you'll end up old and alone and you haven't had a date in this millennium; (8) you're not that attracted to a guy, but he seems to potentially be great boyfriend/husband/father/provider material and maybe there's more there than meets the eye; (9) a thousand other reasons, too numerous to mention here. The point is, there are a host of motivations that prompt you to go on a date. We, on the other hand, have only one: We want to get laid.

"Oh come on," you say, "sometimes guys just want to get to know us better." No, they don't. We already know everything we need to know to take you on a date. We *know* we find you attractive. We *know* that for one or more reasons of your own you've agreed to go out with us. And we *know* that we want to be plowing your fields at our earliest opportunity. That is the sum total of our knowledge and that's good enough for us.

"Okay, I understand you like our outsides," you counter, "but don't you want to get to know what we're like on the inside, too?" Yes, and we hope that before the night is over we'll know what you're like inside as a result of having been there. We're optimistic that way. For us, a first date is like any other date. We hope that by the end we've sweated up the sheets together. Doesn't that make us shallow? By women's standards, perhaps. But by our standards, it just makes us … men.

Perhaps at this point you're thinking I'm dead wrong. Your boyfriend/fiancé/husband/baby daddy isn't like that. He was intrigued by your wit and intelligence and didn't even make a move on you for several dates/weeks/months. (If he waited longer than months, why exactly were *you* seeing *him*?) While he may have found your sterling conversation amusing, the sad truth is he was just biding his time until he worked up the nerve to take action. And all the time you were talking to him, he was barely listening, imagining you naked and trying to figure out when he would finally have the guts to see firsthand just how accurate his imagination was.

And herein lies the greatest irony of the whole dating experience. Women generally like to stretch out the dating process, postponing having sex with us until they feel comfortable that they really know who we are. But our goal is primarily to get you in the sack, so we'll say just about anything we think you want to hear to get us to the Promised Land. Thus, you're not really getting to know us at all. You're getting to know the persona we think is most likely to expedite our journey to your vagina. And we're not getting to know you either, because we're so focused on achieving our objective that we could easily miss just how great you really are. And since you've spent so much time "getting to know us," by the time you do finally spread your legs, you're likely to already have feelings for us. Which is truly a shame since in many cases, before you have sex with us, we don't even really know if we *like* you.

Shocking? Perhaps. But because sex means so much to us, until we get to know one of your most important facets, your sexuality, we're not sure how we feel about you. Of course, that really isn't an issue as long as we enjoy our intimate interlude with you. But what if the sex is bad or something about you in bed is a total turnoff? Fortunately we're not that hard to please, so that doesn't happen that often. But when it does ... "Houston, we've got a problem." Now you're emotionally invested and we've discovered we don't want to see you again. Why do we feel this way? Because we were just hanging in until we had sex with you so we could find out whether or not we liked you. And you can't blame us for not wanting to continue seeing you if we don't like you. After all, you wouldn't continue seeing us if you felt similarly. And were you not already emotionally invested in us, you'd just as likely kick us to the curb if the sex sucked or something about us hugely disgusted you.

The problem is that in your attempt to protect your heart by waiting to have sex, you have all but guaranteed heartbreak if, in fact, we find the sexual chemistry sub par and therefore stop seeing you. And this unfortunate situation is the basis for one of the biggest myths concerning men: "He just dated me till he got what he wanted." Absolutely not true. With rare exception, men don't spend significant amounts of time and money on women just so they can have sex with them *once* and move on. Yes, we want to have sex with you, but we hope like hell that we have a good time, because now all our efforts have paid off and we have someone we can probably have sex with on a regular basis. And that makes us and our penises really happy. Plus, now that we know sex with you is good, we suddenly are even more attracted to you. And finally we know we actually *like* you. So we're apt to want to repeat our liaisons ad infinitum, while potentially emotionally investing in you as well.

So, let's review, shall we? With the exception of relatives and some business associates, men only ask you out because they want to have sex with you. They lie to you about virtually everything until you sleep with them, and it is only at that point that they finally decide whether they like you or not. See, I told you dating could be a major source of confusion, frustration, and angst. Unfortunately, nobody has come up with a viable alternative to this awkward enterprise, so at least for now, we have to grin and bear it (and we hope, very quickly, grin and *bare* it). And not that I'm pushing this agenda (I'm married, so it does me no good), but do reconsider the wisdom of procrastinating going to bed with the guy you're dating. I'm not saying you should jump into bed with him right away (although that would be *my* desire if *we* were dating), but don't wait so long that you're devastated if he kicks you to the curb soon after you *do* get intimate. On the other hand, that is unlikely to happen, since now that you've read this book and have learned how to be an irresistible, sexual dynamo, you're likely to rock any guy's world.

I have one final dating note and it concerns the issue of male "friends." "Why would you bring them up in a chapter about dating?" you ask. "Yes, we go out, but they're not really dates because they're not interested in me sexually." How wrong you are. Unless they're gay, most guys that want to go out and spend one-on-one time with you actually want to *go in* and spend "one-on-one" time with you. At least they *did* at some point in time in your relationship, whether you knew it or not. And just because they've never acted on it, doesn't mean they aren't lusting after you in their hearts. It just means they don't have the guts, the know-how, or what they perceived as the ideal opportunity to make their move. And if you're really convinced that your male friends don't think of you that way, invite them to have sex with you and see what they say. Assuming both of you are unattached, their answer is very likely to be muffled as they frantically pull their shirt over their head.

CHAPTER NINE

Men and Masturbation

You should know from the get-go that *not* all men masturbate. Only males of the species that possess some level of consciousness and a functioning penis are apt to exercise their God-given right to play with themselves. And it's not only in your guy's distant past. Another "dirty little secret" is that men continue to "pull their puds" to one degree or another even *after* they become sexually active with you. This includes boyfriends, live-in lovers, and even husbands. No matter how much we're getting from you, occasionally there still comes a time when a man takes matters into his own hands. (Where do you think that expression *came* from?) It is also important to set the record straight as to *why* men pleasure themselves. Contrary to what you may believe, your man's masturbatory habits have absolutely nothing to do with his satisfaction (or lack thereof) with your joint sex life. In fact, it isn't about you at all. It's quite simply about a guy and his penis, man's *true* best friend. (Sorry, Rover. I know you can fetch, roll over, and drink from the toilet, but really it's no contest.) And though straight men have no interest in another dude's equipment, we can become downright sentimental about our own protuberances.

The bottom line is this: We stroke ourselves because it's what we've always done since we first discovered the pleasure and relief it brought. A long time ago, when we were awkward and acne-ridden and nobody else would have sex with us, our hand and our penis developed a very close working relationship. And it's good that they did, because were it not for their harmonious cooperation, most of us would have shuffled through our teens with permanent pup tents in our pants. And though our ultimate target was your nether regions, our autoerotic manipulations allowed us to efficiently relieve the pressure in our congested loins.

So why do we still masturbate now that we have a sexual partner with whom we can frolic? The answer is quite simple: There are times when you're unavailable, not in the mood, too tired, or sick. And rather than deprive ourselves of sexual release, we return to the tried-and-true, dependable habit of our youth. It allows us to remain faithful and monogamous while still giving ourselves a "happy ending." And while you might question why we can't just wait until you're ready for action, the truth is there's no good reason why we *should*. We're not cheating on you; we're ministering to our own needs. Sure, we'd rather *you* were ministering to our needs, but we're practical if nothing else. And when we're horny, frustrated, tense, or just can't sleep and your vagina's on a coffee break, we exercise the self-reliance we developed so long ago. It's actually advantageous to you. If you think we're sexually persistent now, imagine how we'd be if we had to depend solely upon you for every ejaculation. So essentially, our jerking off is our way of respecting your space and giving your sensitive spot a little "R and R." And while I'm not claiming that our "beating our meat" is purely altruistic ("making the world better through masturbation"), I do believe it makes us a little less grumpy. So at least in some small way we're contributing to domestic harmony. And given that, could world peace be far behind?

CHAPTER TEN

What Men Want out of Their Relationship with You

As you now know, men are fairly simple and straightforward in their use of language and in their general wants and needs. Relationships are no exception. Men look to the women they are romantically involved with for sex, comfort, and companionship—usually in that order. We're not looking for respect, financial help, security, or advice about our career, wardrobe, or dietary choices. We want to be with you because we like spending time with you. That's it.

I know this must sound unbelievably obvious, but it is nonetheless true. Men are fairly self-sufficient when it comes to the day-to-day adventures of ordinary life. We are socialized to make decisions and resolve our own problems without feedback or consensus. We fully expect to be responsible for our own financial security and that of our families. We act when we are moved to do so and rarely spend too much time contemplating all the "What ifs." While that is also true of some women, these attitudes and behaviors are virtually universal in guys.

Because of our pragmatic self-reliance, we look to you to be our oasis from the sometimes harsh realities of the world. That's what I mean by "comfort." It's not that we want continuous soothing words, massage on demand, or the soft cushion of your breasts to lay our weary head upon (okay we do want

that—weary heads *love* boobs). The fact is that we want to be
with you because you enhance our own little personal piece of
the world. And you make us feel better about ourselves. And
the better you make us feel about us, the better we feel about
you. (Conversely, the more you berate or ridicule us, the worse
we feel about you and our relationship. But this is about what
we are looking *for* in a relationship, so no need to focus on the
negative.)

Then there's the matter of sex. I've already spent a great
deal of time pontificating on its importance to us. Suffice it to
say, sexual activity is at the top-of-the-list of what we look for
in an intimate relationship. And while this may offend or an-
noy you, it is still absolutely true. And though we can take care
of ourselves sexually, we prefer the comfort of a slippery vagina
to that of our sweaty palms. See "comfort" again.

Finally, we're looking for companionship. Are you a cool
chick? Are you fun to hang out with? Do we like to do similar
things in our spare time? All these things are important to our
wanting to spend large amounts of time with you. Sure, we can
have fun with our friends, but they rarely stroke our ego and
never our penis, so your company is definitely preferable.

You are probably asking yourself about our long term goals
for a relationship. Perhaps you even believed *that* was what
this chapter was going to be about, but the truth is, prior to
age twenty-eight or twenty-nine, most guys have *no* plans or
goals for their relationships. They are simply enjoying your
company, your wit, and your body. The fact that many men
get married before that time is less a result of what *they* had
planned, and more a product of their significant other's goals
and desires. Yes, there *are* guys that are anxious to "settle down"
and get married as teenagers, but they're a relative rarity, and
an overwhelming majority of them are divorced before they
even reach their mid-twenties. Men don't naturally start seriously contemplating the future of their romantic relationships

until they're finished with their education and settled into their careers. It is at that point that something clicks in our brain that signals us that it may be time to start looking for a mate. Though not all men receive this wake-up call, those who do are often surprised by how it reshapes the way they approach relationships. For the first time, they may actually consider "where this relationship is going" and "if we're going to take this to the next level," both questions they previously avoided like a chick flick marathon or a knee to the groin.

And having reached this turning point in their lives, what do men now look for in the women with whom they are considering commingling their assets and their DNA? Sure some men look for a solid partner and a good mother for their children. And yes, we try to find a woman we can imagine spending the rest of our lives with, one we believe has goals and aspirations similar to our own. But most of us are looking for someone to regularly be physically intimate with, someone to sooth us when we're tired and stressed, someone fun to spend time with. In other words, we're looking for sex, comfort, and companionship ... because, to us, that is the very definition of "happily ever after." And you can't blame us for wanting that, can you?

CHAPTER ELEVEN

What Men Find Attractive

We have already talked a great deal about men's motivations and perceptions, and in that regard this chapter may deal with some things we have previously touched on. It is my intent now, however, to explore those things that men find particularly attractive and conversely those things that repulse us and cause our testicles to withdraw to the protective shelter of our abdominal cavities.

It is important to again remind you that these things are what *men* find attractive. They are not presented as what *is* attractive or what *you* find attractive or even what *should be* attractive. This is strictly informational. It is not meant to exhort you to change anything about yourself for any reason ... unless, of course, you want men to find you appealing on some level. If that's the case, pay close attention. If not, carry on and don't change a thing. There. You have my disclaimer. Proceed at your own risk.

As I've mentioned before, men like women for a variety of reasons, but primarily because they are different from us, especially in the physical sense. It is, in fact, this structural dissimilarity that causes our hearts to race and our groins to tingle. The more unlike us you are in the way you look, the better. Whether we are accurate in our assessment or not, we perceive ourselves as being hard, lean, muscular, and angular.

We expect to have body hair adorn our limbs, underarms, pubic area, chest, and face. In contrast to this, we anticipate that you will be soft and curvy, and with the exception of your nether regions and your head, be virtually hair-free. This is not to say that if you have a boyish figure or hairy toes that we will not be drawn to you. It simply means that the further you stray from our perception of the "feminine ideal," the less inclined we are to want to play doctor with you … at least while we're sober. After a few drinks, you could resemble a hirsute Winston Churchill and we'd probably still do ya.

Over the years, I have had many women complain to me that men don't seem to notice them or approach them with romantic intentions. Almost without exception, this has been because of how these women dressed. Despite the fact that most of them were good-looking, they unintentionally clothed themselves to obscure this fact. And this caused men to pass over them as they scanned the room for potential paramours. Why? Because men are visually oriented, and when they look at women, they see what is obvious and apparent. If a woman is wearing something shapeless or conservative, a man's eyes will quickly move on. What we are looking for either consciously or subconsciously is someone who (1) looks *obviously* feminine and (2) is likely to have sex with us before we have to shave again. Therefore, if you are dressed modestly, we assume sex is not going to be on the table (or any other piece of furniture) in the foreseeable future. And whether or not you're a wild woman under your baggy frock is completely inconsequential: If you dress like a pilgrim, the geography of your petticoats is going to remain unexplored territory and the only "stuffing" you're likely to be grateful for at Thanksgiving is that which came out of the hind end of the turkey.

"Okay, so how would *you* like me to dress?" I hear you inquire with an air of annoyance and disdain. Well, since you asked nicely, I'll tell you: As sluttishly as possible. And what do I mean by that? Dress in a manner that shows off whatever you have to its best advantage. Show the maximum amount of skin you can get away with without having to be pixilated for broadcast television. Display oodles of cleavage. If you aren't opulently blessed, wear something tight that will showcase your nipples. Show off your belly if you don't have too much of one. Wear something that hugs your ass, as long as local ordinances won't require you display the warning CAUTION: WIDE LOAD. Let 'em see your legs, preferably in form-flattering heels. If you wear a dress, show some thigh. In other words, dress in a manner that would provoke your father to ground you for the rest of your adult life.

I can hear some of you questioning the wisdom of this. After all, you are a professional and should dress as such. Yes, you should … when your work environment demands it. The key is to dress appropriately to the situation. The stylish business suit you wear at the office is perfectly acceptable when you're in a board meeting, crunching numbers, or handling client accounts. But when you go out with the express intent of meeting eligible guys in a social setting, it is equally important to wear the proper garb: something that registers in a guy's mind that you are (1) a woman and (2) ready for a good time (whatever that may be). The best gauge of what constitutes appropriate man-meeting attire is this: If your female friends would call it chic, stylish, elegant, stunning, or sophisticated, it's all wrong. Men you encounter will give a collective yawn. If, however, your friends would label it trampy, trashy, whorish, or scandalous, you're on the right track.

Now, if you're like my many female friends, you're thinking, "Yeah, I'll attract attention dressed like that, but the only kind of guy I'll attract is one who's only interested in having sex with me." Exactly. Because if you've been paying attention at all up to this point, that's the only kind of guy there is! Until we have sex with you, that *is* our only interest. After that, when we finally get to know you as a person, the fact that you were provocatively dressed when we first saw you will have no bearing on the future of our relationship. Consider your sexy attire equivalent to a movie preview—It's the thing that catches our attention and gets us into the theater. Once there, our opinion of that particular film will be solely based upon our enjoyment of the movie, not the trailer that drew us in. And if we really enjoy the experience, we'll be grateful that the advertisement that lured us in was so effective. It's win-win for your relationship and all but guarantees a healthy box-office.

Okay, let's talk about your hair. The simple truth is we like lots of it. *We* may have bald spots and receding hairlines, but we find you most appealing when your locks are long and flowing. Color, texture, and style are insignificant to us. Frankly, the less you do to it, the more we like it. That just-got-out-of-bed look is actually appealing because we optimistically interpret it as a ready-to-get-back-into-bed quaff. And there is nothing hotter to the male libido than the sight of a woman in a convertible with her long tresses blowing in the wind. That epitomizes youth and femininity—two things that get us hot.

"Aha!" you say. "*Youth*. Men only like *young* women." Not true. A woman doesn't have to be young for us to like her, but young-looking is definitely more appealing than matronly. Unfortunately there is a tradition in this country of women chopping off their hair as they age. It may be more convenient and less work to have shorter hair, but it's also far less feminine from a guy's perspective. And "less feminine" translates into "less attractive." But the absolute worst thing you can do for your looks is adopt an "old lady helmet hairdo." You know what I'm talking about. It's the stiff, short, teased, precisely trimmed, on-top-of-your-head style that transforms otherwise attractive women into Grandma. And as much as we love Grandma, we are fairly repulsed by the idea of getting naked with her.

Now we move to a very sensitive area … your weight. And although men have very definite ideas on this, in general, a man's ideal weight for a woman is considerably higher than a woman's ideal weight for herself or her peers. In other words, *we* like you meatier than *you* like you. While we like you to be "in shape" our definition of that is significantly different from your own. And it's no wonder. While we fantasize about the shapely, curvy, voluptuous models in beer ads, you take your weight cues from the rail-thin, waif-like models you see in fashion magazines. Those women scare us! Sure they have beautiful faces, but you can count their vertebrae from across the room. An enthusiastic romp in the sack might cause them multiple fractures. And bones cracking during sex is a major turnoff.

The truth is, as long as you're proportional (or hwp, as they say on Craigslist), and your waist is smaller than your hips, you can carry a few extra pounds and we'll probably find it sexy. Remember, we like you soft and curvy. Toned is fine, but ripped and muscular just makes us feel bad about ourselves. And if you have "pecs" where you should have breasts, don't expect to be starring in any of our wet dreams (like that's what you aspire to anyway).

At this point, I have a not-so-quick comment about obesity. It is currently an epidemic in this country. While we like you to be shapely, curvy, maybe even a little "thick," only the fetishist seeks out an excessively heavy woman. If your weight is twice what the health charts say it should be, most men will likely perceive you as unhealthful and thus not seek you out. Perhaps it's part of our genetic imprinting to be attracted to the fittest females and conversely put off by those we view as being way-too-skinny or too over-stuffed. And cruel as it may be, if you fall into the obese category, the guys who *do* sleep with you will probably go out of their way to hide it from their friends. Sure, you might be a warm, wet place to cradle their

David M. Matthews

penis, but actually be seen in public with you? Not a chance. Is that fair? No. Is it right? Not at all. But it's how it is. And wishing things were different doesn't change the reality of how they actually are. You may be an exceptional person, but guys are visually oriented, and if your waist disappeared a hundred pounds ago, all we see is rolls of blobbish flesh. And that's about as appealing to us as it sounds. Even if *we* look like we swallowed another person whole, we generally like our women to appear less like a pachyderm in stature. It is perhaps similar to our feelings about those brittle-looking Vogue models, except instead of being scared of inadvertently hurting *them*, we are concerned about you accidentally crushing *us* (or at least some vital part of us). Neither scenario is particularly arousing to men, other than those with a sadistic or masochistic streak. And are *those* the guys you really want to hang out with? But enough said. Be happy with who you are, and if you're not, do something about it. And should you decide to leave the realm of the obese, rejoice in the fact that not only will your heart and your knees thank you, but your self-esteem will be giving you deep tongue kisses. Could attractive guys be far behind?

CHAPTER TWELVE

Answers to Your Questions about Men

Just so you don't think I'm writing this book in a vacuum (which would be noisy and rather dusty, I would guess), I have asked a selection of women of different ages, ethnicities, backgrounds, and geographical locations "what confounds you most about the enigmatic male of the species?" The following is a small sampling of their astoundingly numerous questions.

Question: How do guys just shut off their emotions?

Answer: They don't. They simply don't talk about them, show them, or explore them in any public or private way. Men feel deeply, but since they have been taught to suppress any feelings or vulnerability, they simply internalize everything, except anger, an emotion society deems socially acceptable. And although you might *think* you want your man to "open up" and show you more emotions, is that truly what you desire? Do you really want to hear him tell you about his insecurities, doubts, and fears? Do you want to know why he tears up every time he hears "Puff the Magic Dragon"? Do you think you could possibly respect him if you found out that deep down he was more of an emotional wreck than you? Doubtful. And even if you could accept those things without consciously judging him, *subconsciously* you would probably feel he was somewhat less of a man than you previously thought he was.

And at that moment, your guy suddenly and without warning becomes ever-so-slightly less attractive to you. And we inherently know that. So since being attractive to you is important to us, because it potentially leads to sex, we will continue to guard our feelings as fanatically as we guard our testicles. And you know how careful we are with *them*.

Question: Is it possible for a guy to like a girl if he thinks she doesn't like him but she does?

Answer: Absolutely. A guy is not motivated to like you or not based on anything other than if he is attracted to you. But be warned: Even if he isn't particularly attracted to you, if you let on that you like *him*, he may well respond very positively. Not necessarily because he honestly likes *you*, but because your liking him will most likely lead to your having sex with him. And having sex is something he most certainly likes.

Question: Why do guys like to be really close friends with girls but nothing more?

Answer: They don't. With few exceptions, all the males you know as "friends" would sleep with you in a minute given the least little bit of encouragement, unless they're very religious, in a committed relationship, or gay. And even then, given the right circumstances and a little alcohol … their penis is likely to make an appearance.

In truth, guys don't really want you as friends in the traditional sense of friendship. They hang out with you because they are attracted to you and want to find their way under your thong. It's not that they don't appreciate your company—they may. But they'd appreciate it more if it included humping.

"But what about all the guys I hang out with who've never given any indication they are interested in me *that* way?" you ask. There's a simple explanation for that. All those guys just don't have the guts, the nerve, the *cajones* to make their move.

They want you, but they are too wimpy to do anything about it. So they hang out with you day after day, week after week, year after year, hoping you will either make a move on them or that someday they'll grow a spine that will work in conjunction with their currently nonfunctioning testicles. But don't hold your breath. It ain't likely to happen any time soon.

Question: Why do "grown up" guys like to play video games so much?

Answer: This apparent mystery can easily be explained by a simple syllogism: Video games are fun. Guys like to have fun. Therefore, guys like video games. That's all there is to it. You understand that girls just want to have fun—well, in that way men and women are alike. Only instead of shopping, dancing, and dishing with our friends, we like to compete with each other and blow things up. And thankfully video games allow us to do that while drinking a brew and avoiding a visit from Homeland Security.

Question: Do most guys judge girls based only on physical appearance?

Answer: Yup. To us, initially at least, how you look is paramount to physical attraction. Fortunately, not all guys are attracted to the *same* physical attributes so a wide variety of looks still fall within the category of "attractive." It is this assortment of tastes that allows us to classify such a diverse group of women as Marilyn Monroe, Cleopatra, Kate Moss and Ariel, The Little Mermaid, all as beauties. And although you may think it superficial that we put so much emphasis on your appearance, it's how we're hardwired. And once we get to know you, other things enter into the equation: how much fun you are to spend time with; how you make us feel about ourselves; how hot you are in bed; how easy you are to get along with. Even if we are lukewarm to you initially in the looks department, excelling at any of these other areas will increase your desirability factor substantially. Bottom line is that it's your exterior that gets you noticed but your interior that keeps us coming back for more. (That sounds like a double entendre, but it's true, whether you take it at face value or allow your dirty mind to consider the alternate, naughty possibilities.)

Question: Is it a turn-off if girls make the first move?

Answer: Hell no! Only a very young, extremely religious, or really insecure guy is put off by a woman taking the romantic initiative (unless he's gay or finds you repulsive). The rest of us love it when you give us an obvious sign you're into us. But the keyword here is "obvious." Subtlety is usually lost on us. So if you want to make the first move, do it in such a way that we can have only one interpretation of what your intent is. Smoldering looks and coquettish eye-batting are best left to classic movie sirens. Be clear and be direct. Get close. Touch us. Stroke our hair … and then do something *obvious*. Because, in our sometimes-clueless minds, we may perceive even these actions as you just being friendly. I know it's hard to believe, but trust me, I know whereof I speak. It takes you doing or saying something overt to really get the point across. *Don't say*, "I like spending time/hanging out with you." That tells us nothing—you could be saying that to your old-maid aunt or your finicky cat, Mister Whiskers. Make it crystal clear where your head is at. *Do say*, "You've got very sensual lips. I bet you're a great kisser." Then take the initiative and find out. It's hard for even the densest among us to misinterpret a wet, probing tongue in our mouth. And there are obviously much more X-rated things you could say or do to help him get the message, but the bottom line is your direct approach will yield favorable results an overwhelming majority of the time.

Question: Why can't men put the damn toilet seat back down after they use it?

Answer: They can, but why should they? When was the last time you left the toilet seat *up* so that it was ready for our urinary needs? True, it doesn't take much for us to lower the seat so it is ready for you, but it takes relatively the *same* amount of effort for you to raise the seat so that it is convenient for us. Consideration works both ways. But truthfully, how hard is it to be responsible for positioning the toilet seat so that it is suited to your particular needs and letting the next user behave similarly? And the argument that you might inadvertently "fall in" because the previous occupant left the seat up, really doesn't hold much water. (No pun intended. Well, maybe a little …) Don't you look before you sit? I do … *because I may have left the seat up last time and I don't want an unscheduled derriere dunk.* I think the key here is "look before you leak." If we can all agree to do that, then nobody has to end up with soggy buns.

So there it is. Some of the more vexing questions about men answered. But I didn't address an issue that's been bugging you for years? Well, there's still hope. Email me at david@ everymanseesyounaked.com and I'll try to answer some of the more universally baffling questions I receive in my next book or upcoming newspaper/Internet column. The answers are out there … just send me the questions!

CHAPTER THIRTEEN

A Quiz: Test Your "Man-Q"

The following ten questions gauge whether you've been paying attention so far or not. Good luck!

1. A guy you're friendly with at work invites you to grab a drink with him one night as you're leaving the office. His motivation for this is

   a. You're fun at work and he wants to get to know you better.
   b. He knows you're a good listener and he has some work-related issues he wants to get off his chest.
   c. He thinks of you as a bud and just wants to hang out.
   d. He's hoping that after a few margaritas he'll get to lick that ice cream cone tattoo on your inner thigh.

2. You ask your husband where he wants to go out to dinner tonight and he responds, "I don't care." What he really means is

   a. He's annoyed that after a hard day at work he has to go back out again.
   b. Any restaurant will be fine.
   c. He has a specific cuisine in mind, but doesn't want to seem pushy.

    d. He wants Chinese or Mexican, and knows you prefer, Italian, but hopes that if he doesn't specify a particular choice you might suggest one of his preferences and he can magnanimously go along with it *and* earn brownie points for being so agreeable.

3. You have your stylist cut your long hair and turn it into a short, stylish, low-maintenance do. When you ask your husband what he thinks, he replies, "Why'd you cut your hair?" What he means is
    a. "I hate it."
    b. "I was used to your longer hair, but this new cut is very chic."
    c. "Oh, God, you're turning into your mother."
    d. "Oh, God, you're turning into *my* mother."

4. A guy you've had a crush on for a long time finally asks you out. You want to impress him on the date, so you …
    a. dress to show off your exquisite taste in clothing.
    b. dress to show off your exquisite body.
    c. pepper the conversation with examples of how independent and self-sufficient you are.
    d. pepper the conversation with how financially successful and career-oriented you are.

5. Your guy accidentally lets it slip how attractive he thinks Scarlett Johansson is. What he really means is
    a. She's pretty and sexy and you're a cow.
    b. She's pretty and sexy and you could never, ever, possibly satisfy him as long as that bitch is alive.
    c. She's pretty and sexy and he's hoping you'll pick up on the fact that he's dissatisfied with your relation-

ship and is trying to let you down softly so that he might be free to pursue his beloved Scarlett.

    d. She's pretty and sexy and it has absolutely nothing to do with you.

6. You've been dating a guy for three months and have successfully kept from having sex with him. These days, when you two go out, he no longer pressures you for sex. What's behind his attitude change?
   a. He's grown to respect your resolve, and he realizes that if he wants you, he'll just have to be patient.
   b. He finally got the message that you're not ready for sex and he's cool with it.
   c. He realizes the wisdom in waiting and knows that when you two finally *do* have sex the wait will have been worth it.
   d. He's getting it somewhere else.

7. At the end of your first date with a new guy, he says, "I'll call you." What does he mean?
   a. He had a good time and he wants to ask you out again.
   b. It's the end of the date and it's his way of saying "good-night."
   c. He had a terrible time and he wants to torture you for it by causing you to sit expectantly night after night waiting by the phone.
   d. Quit being so analytical. He's a man and men speak literally, so what he means is *he will call you.*

8. You finally sleep with the guy you've been dating for six weeks and you never hear from him again. The reason is
   a. Men are bastards. He was just using you 'til he got what he wanted.

b. Men are bastards. Now that you've "given up the goods," he no longer respects you.

c. Men are bastards. He was unimpressed with your sexual performance and now interest in you has waned.

d. After having sex with you he realized he's gay … but he's a man, so he's still a bastard.

9. You just had a highly emotional break-up with your boyfriend of three years and a week later you hear he's hot and heavy with some woman he met at step class. This proves that

a. He never really loved you.

b. He really loved you and this is his way of dealing with his pain and loss.

c. He's an emotionally immature horndog who can't go a week without "dipping his wick."

d. He has a thing for well-toned, sweaty women.

10. Which of the following statements is *not* true?

a. Men don't read self-help books.

b. Men cheat because they get the opportunity.

c. Every man sees you naked.

d. Men think all pregnant women are beautiful.

So how do you think you did? Pretty well? Okay, let's take a look at the correct answers.

Question 1: d. Generally speaking, when a guy asks you out for some "one-on-one" time, it's because he wants to intermingle bodily fluids with you. Don't be deceived by the fact that he's a friendly co-worker. If he wanted to swap stories or pick your brain, he'd do it on a coffee/lunch/smoke break. Drinks are liquid lubrication, and he means to use them to help your underwear glide effortlessly down your legs.

Question 2: b. Even though *you* may almost always have a preference that you don't verbalize, the same is probably not true of your man. If he says that he doesn't care, accept him at his word and revel in the fact that you now get to satisfy your unusual craving for sauerkraut and sushi (if you can find a Japanese beer garden).

Question 3: a. This is one of the very few instances when men don't often say exactly what they feel. After many centuries of learning when women ask about their appearance, what they usually want is an affirmation, men have finally started to wise up … a little. They've learned to avoid a direct answer, if their truthful response will provoke anger, tears, or exile to the living room couch. So they've developed a less-confrontational "question-answer." Not really definitive, it preemptively takes your temperature on how *you* feel about the specific attribute in question. This allows them to get your input on how they should respond, while offering them a moment to repress some visceral, almost involuntary outburst that will most-certainly eliminate "a little nookie" from tonight's bill-of-fare.

And why does he hate your chic new bob? Because, for men, long hair epitomizes femininity, youth, and sexuality. And cutting your hair short represents a rejection of all those things. So don't expect us to embrace your effort to become an asexual old crone. And yes, so you know, when you "chop your locks," you *do* tend to remind us of your mother, or worse, ours. And trust me when I tell you that that image doesn't exactly make us want to throw you down and make wild, passionate monkey-love to you.

Question 4: b. Men are visual, so "show 'em what you ya got," "if you got it flaunt it," or any number of other clichés that embody the premise that it pays to advertise. If we like what we see (and generally the more we see, the more we like), we're very likely to want to see more of you (in more ways than one). Telling us that you're self-sufficient and independent may sound like a plus to you, but to us it seems like you don't really need us and you'll be given to reminding us of that fact on an annoyingly regular basis. So, all in all, not real appealing. And while *you* might be impressed with your stylish garb and financial success, it means virtually nothing to us. The only assets of yours that we really care about are the fleshy kinds that feel good pressed up against us.

Question 5: d. No matter how exquisite a creature you are, your man is still going to be attracted to other women. And while he'd be wise to keep the specifics of his "lusting in his heart" to himself, the prurient thoughts about other women will nonetheless continue to bombard his consciousness. The important things to remember are (1) It's automatic and he can't help it; (2) thinking is not doing, so he's not guilty of being unfaithful; (3) his attraction to Scarlett is unlikely to be reciprocated; and (4) she's just the object of his fantasy. *You* are the object of his *love*. And if you had to choose between the two, wouldn't you rather be the latter than the former?

Question 6: d. Let's review. Guys date you because they want to have sex with you. If after a reasonable amount of time (what *he* thinks is reasonable), you're still avoiding having sex with him, he will look elsewhere. Why wouldn't he? *You* may think you're worth waiting for, but he has no reason to feel that way. After all, if you're this unwilling to become sexually intimate with him, it just might be an indication of a myriad of issues and inhibitions, none of which bode well for a satisfying sexual encounter (when and if that ever happens).

So why is he continuing to spend time with you? Because men are inherently optimistic, and he reasons that one day, when all the stars and planets align just right, you may deign to have sex with him. Just know that in the interim, some other woman is likely to be working her way into his heart the more that he works his way into her pants. That's not to say that you should alter *your* behavior. You just need to be aware of the realities of the situation: Men crave sexual contact. Deprive them of it long enough and they'll find it elsewhere.

Question 7: b. This is a tricky one because it is an exception to the "men say exactly what they mean" rule (although, technically, this *is* usually prior to any sexual activity, so truthfulness is not a guy's top priority). The end of a date is a particularly stressful time for a man. If the evening has gone well and he's still interested in you, the time has now arrived for him to make his move and try to get you to be as physically intimate as he can. (Even if he *isn't* that interested in you, as long as he's not totally repulsed by you, getting you naked is still probably up there on his "to do" list.) But there is a high degree of probability that he will fall far short of his goal. And there's an always-possible outcome of being pushed away, slapped, seriously laughed-at, or most humiliatingly, being given the cheek. So with the possibility of abject failure looming large, the pressure is on. It is therefore no surprise that under these circumstances, a man's ability to give a pithy, honest, and appropriate farewell might be greatly diminished. This is especially true if he is recovering from the disappointment of a quick peck or a close encounter with your face flesh. At this point he realizes the date is over and he must find some quick way to extricate himself and his battered self-esteem. Saying "good-night," "see ya around," or "ciao" seems a bit abrupt. And if he's still desirous of seeking out your company in the future, "later, bitch" is probably not apropos. So instead he reaches into his bag of innocuously vague platitudes and comes up with the concise, face-saving, optimistic-sounding chestnut, "I'll call you." But truthfully, at that moment, all he really means is "good-bye."

He is now free to beat a hasty retreat, nurse his injured ego (along with a fifth of tequila), and figure out whether or not he wants to see you again, forget you, or swear off women he doesn't have to inflate.

Question 8: c. The truth is that men don't really know if they like you or not until after they've had sex with you. Prior to that, all we're focused on is gaining access to that steamy sanctuary between your thighs. So now, for the first time, post-coitus, we're actually "seeing" you. If we like who you are and/or you were incredible in the sack, we will definitely be back for more. However, if we find your personality less than appealing *and* your sexual performance lacking, it's now time for us to seriously consider the following: (1) Is the probability of repeated, marginally satisfying physical intimacy worth the investment of time and energy? And is this causing us to miss out on opportunities to hook up with someone we'd *really* like? (2) Could we possibly get to like you if we gave it more time? (Maybe you're a quick learner and with proper encouragement your sexual performance might improve. Then perhaps we could talk you into a ménage a trois.) (3) If we continue to be physically involved with you, are we unfairly implying some level of "relationship advancement" that doesn't really exist? And when you discover this, will you be emotionally devastated and/or come after our genitalia with power tools (and not the good kind)? As you can see, some weighty issues. And you thought guys had no substance. Of course we do. And we'd be happy to show you more of it if you'll have a threesome with us.

Question 9: b. Unlike women, men have no network of emotional support. We can't talk to our friends and family about our feelings, because we don't want to be thought of as wimps. And eating massive quantities of marshmallow fluff only makes us feel sticky and a little gassy. So in our pragmatic wisdom, we do the only thing we know will definitely help us ease our aching heart—find someone new. And fast. You see, the greater the pain, the more urgent the need to quell it. So it's either find a new woman to make us forget our pain or crawl inside a bottle of Maker's Mark. And a new woman is less likely to make us hug the toilet or forget where we parked our Beemer.

Question 10: d. Sorry, it's true. The man whose seed you're carrying may find your newly rounded profile appealing, but those of us who didn't knock you up view you with less-adoring eyes. It's not that we find you repulsive—we'd still do you if the opportunity presented itself. But perceive you as beautiful simply because you have a baby bump? Hardly. And before you trot out Demi Moore and her engorged belly on the cover of *Vanity Fair* as proof of the sexy appeal of a woman with a bun in the oven, remember this: (1) Men don't read *Vanity Fair* (at least not *straight* men). (2) Demi's so hot, Robert Redford paid a million dollars just to have sex with her one time (in *Indecent Proposal*, anyway). Has Bob called you with any similar offer? (3) How many times have you seen that particular pose on any guy's screen saver (except for perhaps, Bruce Willis'— the baby daddy)? It's not that we have anything against pregnant women. It's just that a swollen stomach doesn't suddenly transform a woman into a universal state of gorgeousness (although we do applaud the accompanying engorged breasts). Your pregnant belly isn't offensive, but it also isn't fine art. And for those who'll argue it's "God's art" because it's his creation, don't forget he also created warts, pus, and hemorrhoids. And you'd be hard-pressed to argue the beauty of those physical amenities.

So, for better or worse, those are your answers. And what would a quiz be without a chart to rate your enlightenment on a completely subjective and arbitrary scale? It just wouldn't be American ... or *Cosmopolitan*. Hence, I have created the following to determine your "Man-Q" and show how male-savvy you are.

If you answered 10 correctly: Congratulations, you've been paying attention! Your relationship with the man in your life is likely to be greatly enhanced due to your increased understanding of what makes your significant other tick. He'll love the way you "get" him, and he is likely to show his appreciation with gifts, compliments, and a greater willingness to accompany you to linen sales and the ballet.

If you answered 8–9 correctly: You're exhibiting an admirable working knowledge of the male of the species. And although your understanding isn't perfect, you're well on your way to mastering the "guy code," the first step in laying the foundation for a fulfilling and harmonious relationship. And that's almost as good as chocolate.

If you answered 6–7 correctly: Congratulations, you fall into the C to D grade category. And while this might be a desirable range for cup size, it's not so great as an indicator of what you've learned. So it's time to hunker down and review the material. Pay careful attention to the chapter on sex. It may not improve your test score, but it is sure to make your love life more interesting.

If you answered 0–5 correctly: English isn't your first language, is it? If you're serious about improving your understanding of men, quit multitasking and focus on what's important—reading this extraordinarily well-written treatise on masculine behavioral motivations. Or cram this book under the short leg of a wobbly table and be content with forever fumbling through the jungle of male/female interpersonal interaction. The choice is yours: knowledge or stable furniture.

CHAPTER FOURTEEN

Men and Their Euphemisms

As I mentioned earlier, when it comes to the female form and sexual activity, men have developed an extensive, vivid language of words, expressions, and phrases. Why? Perhaps we just have too much time on our hands. Or maybe it's because we so appreciate sex with you that the contents of Webster's is just entirely too confining. In any case, euphemisms abound. And if you're going to successfully converse with a man on sexual matters, it helps if you have some idea of what he is talking about. As with the previously explored breast synonyms, the following list is ever-growing and by no means comprehensive. Once again, a language advisory is in effect.

By far, our favorite thing to rhapsodize about is what we consider the corporate headquarters of your sexuality, your vagina. It is the altar at which we worship, and mere words seem ill-equipped to adequately convey our consummate enthusiasm for this hallowed orifice and the surrounding neighborhood. Herewith are some examples of our linguistic attempts to canonize the object of our passionate obsession: *bearded clam, beaver, box, canal, cavern, center, chalice, cooch, coochie, cookie, cooter, core, crevice, cunnie, cunt, down there, fanny* (if you're British), *flower, gash, Gates of Heaven, genitals, goods* (as in, "gave up the ..."), *her sex, hole, hot pocket, kitty, kitty cat, love glove* (also slang for *condom*), *lower lips, moist furrow, muff, muffin, muffler, Paradise, passion flower, pleasure portal, poononnie, private parts, privates, pudendum, pussy, quim* (often preceded by the modifier *quivering*), *slice, slit, sluice, snapper, snatch, south of the border, taco, tropical region, tunnel, twat, va-juujj, velvet glove,* and *womanhood.* Whew—some list. I think I need a cigarette … and a cold shower.

Before we move on, it is essential that we not overlook perhaps the most thrilling landmark in the whole vaginal territory, the often-elusive, yet always provocative, chairman-of-the-board of female arousal, the mighty clitoris. Among its many attributes is the odd fact that the clitoris is undoubtedly the most mispronounced of all the female points of interest. And guys are guiltiest of this linguistic faux pas, often referring to this diminutive dynamo as the cli-TOR-is—thus rhyming with Doris and Lavoris, when, as you know, the correct pronunciation is clit' eris—as in the following rhyme: "Tickling her clitoris, set her all a-twitter-ous." Pronounced correctly or not, this tiny organ is so important that it earns an entire euphemistic subset of its own: *Clit, clitty, hot button, love nubbin, man in the boat,* and *pleasure spot.* Sure the list isn't as lengthy as that of the beloved vagina, but perhaps it's correctly proportionate to the amount of relative attention we guys give it.

Next up on the anatomical hit parade is your buttocks. Our fondness for it gave birth to the chestnut, "We hate to see you leave, but we love to watch you go." The following are but a few colorful endearments for the target of our focus whenever you're in front of us: *arse* (if you frequent Renaissance fairs), *ass, back* (as in "Baby's got …"), *backside, behind, booty, bottom, bum* (if you're from the UK), *bumper, buns, butt, caboose, cheeks, cushion, derriere, end, fanny* (unless you're British), *gadoink-gadoink, globes, glutes, kiester, money maker, moon, pooper, rear, rear end, rumble seat, rump, seat, tail* (as in, "piece of …"—which oddly refers to *vaginal penetration,* so go figure), *tokhes* (pronounced took' iss), *tooshie, trunk* (as in, "junk in the ..."), and *tush*. And just a reminder: Like your breasts, so great is our affection for your ass, that "too big" is not usually an issue (see JLo—preferably from behind). As long as your hind quarters (hey, there's another one) aren't so big as to have their own gravitational pull or so small as to make us feel like a pedophile, your sashaying off into the sunset is likely to provoke an appreciative stirring in our shorts.

Now there's the matter of your legs. Though we are universally quite fond of them (most notably when a shapely pair is wrapped around our waist or our neck), these treasured anatomic adornments are inexplicably euphemism-deficient. With the exception of *gams*, which hasn't been part of the contemporary vernacular since the Eisenhower administration, they are simply referred to by their given name. Perhaps I should contact the male powers-that-be and tell them to work on it. In the meantime, we'll have to agree that the divided highway that merges at your crotch, will, until further notice, be uniformly referred to as simply ... *legs*.

And no discussion about men and their euphemisms would be complete without addressing the plethora of pet names we've bestowed upon our most trusted companion—our penis. The following is a colorful representation of our esteemed comrade: *baloney pony, bone, boner, chubby, cock, cocktail frank, dick, dingus, dipstick, dork, drill, dynamo, dong, erection, gun, hard-on, hog, horn, hose, hot dog, javelin, Johnson, John Thomas, joint, kidney prod, kielbasa, lance, little friend, little head, love muscle, magic wand, manhood* (often preceded by the adjective *throbbing*), *meat, member* (in romance novels, preceded by the modifier *tumescent*), *moisture-seeking meat missile, Mister Happy, pecker, peter, peewee, phallus, pile driver, pipe, pleasure stick, poker, pointer, pole, pocket rocket, prick, private parts, privates, prong, pud, pussy prodder, rod, root, salami* (as in "hide the ..."), *sausage, schlong, schmeckle, schmuck, shaft, staff, skin flute, soldier, spear, stiffy, tallywacker, thing, third leg, tool, trouser snake, truncheon, tube steak, wang, weapon, wiener,* and *woody.* Interestingly, if we took away the references to meat products and combat instruments, the list is substantially reduced. I'm not sure what it means, except apparently when we think of our penis, it conjures up imagery of battle and cooked livestock.

And like peanut butter and jelly, ham and cheese, and Siegfried and Roy, one cannot mention the penis without immediately thinking of its faithful ally and crotch co-inhabitant ... the testicles. Our fondness for them is illustrated by the following: *balls, basket, cajones* (Spanish for "balls"), *crotch* (as in "Kick him in the ..."), *family jewels, huevos* (Spanish for "eggs"), *joints, manparts* (as in "Kick him in the ..."), *marbles, nads* (short for *gonads*), *nuts, nutsack, right where it counts* (as in "Kick him ..."), *sack, scrotum,* and *stones* (as in "He's got some ...). Our only wish is that so many of the testicle references weren't preceded by "Kick him in the ..." Oh well, thankfully they make protective cups ... and ice packs.

Moving away from body parts, both his and hers, we come to the actual acts that preoccupy our waking, and often slumbering, thoughts. And it seems most appropriate to begin any discussion of sex acts with the one that's numero uno on guys' list of favorite things ... sexual intercourse. If ever there were a term that cries out for a euphemism, *sexual intercourse* is it. So clinically formal, it makes the act sound about as appealing as a tax audit or a minor amputation. Consequently, a treasure trove of descriptive alternatives have found their way into the popular vernacular: *balling, banging, benefits* (as in, "friends with ..."), *bedding, been with, boffing, boinking, bumping uglies, coitus, connubial bliss, consummation, copulating, dallying, doing it, fucking, getting down, getting it on, getting jiggy, getting some, going all the way, having carnal knowledge, having sex, hitting a homerun, hitting it, hooking up, horizontal mambo, knocking boots, canoodling, knocking one off, knowing each other* (a biblical reference), *laying* (a.k.a. *getting laid*), *making it, making love, making whoopee, marital duty, nailing, nookie, penetration, playing hide-the-salami, plowing the fields, poking, poontang, porking, ravaging, rock and roll* (yes, *that* is where the musical term comes from—one more reason why conservative parents of the 1950s didn't exactly embrace the genre), *screwing, schtupping, scoring, shagging, sleeping with, slipping it to her, The Deed* (as in, "doing …"), *The Nasty,* and *The Old In-And-Out.* A motley group of terms, to be sure, but all of them are better than stinky old *sexual intercourse.* And for those of you who disagree, I say, "sexual intercourse you!"

Now let's talk "oral" (and I don't mean "Roberts"). While men may grumble about you talking too much, you'll never hear them complain about using your mouth in other ways. To put it mildly, men are huge oral sex fans—both getting, and to a lesser extent, giving. As such, the language for this cherished pastime is particularly colorful. Let's start with fellatio (where most men like to start) slang: *blow job, brain salad surgery, deep throating, humjob, hummer, licking his lollipop, mouthing him, polishing his periscope, suck job,* and *swallowing his noodle,* to name just a few. Then there's the colorful cunnilingus collection: *box lunch at the Y, carpet munching, eating out, getting some hair pie, lickety-split, muff diving,* and *mustache ride.* Then, of course, are the terms that are used for *both* forms of lingual love: *French, giving or getting head, giving face, going down,* and the oddly detached-sounding, *oral gratification.* And as I'm sure you're aware, when two people simultaneously engage in mouth-to-genital resuscitation, it is called *69* (not because this is the sixty-ninth position in the Kama Sutra, as some people believe, but because the number is a visual depiction of two people head-to-toe. See, even numbers can be sexy).

And we mustn't forget anal copulation (though some of you might like to), which has its devotees, who fondly refer to this act as: *anal-izing, buggering, butt banging, butt fucking, corn holing*, *fudge packing*, *going in the back door*, *Greek style*, *rear-ending*, *riding the old Hershey Highway*, and the Biblically derived, *sodomizing*. While this certainly isn't everybody's "cup of tea," it's good to know the terms, if for no other reason than to avoid the embarrassment of whipping out a map of Pennsylvania when your lover suggests hitting "the Hershey Highway."

And finally, we come to (cum to?) our national pastime. No, I'm not talking about baseball, although this definitely does involve "choking up on the bat." I am referring to self-love, or masturbation, perhaps the only hobby all men (and according to recent studies, 82% of women—you go, girl) have in common. What follows is a list of our *pet* names (Note: All terms refer to *male* masturbation, except where parenthetically indicated): *autoeroticism* (both), *beating the beaver* (women), *beating your meat*, *beating off*, *choking the chicken*, *dating Mother Palm and her five daughters*, *diddle* (women), *digitizing* (women), *finger banging* (women), *finger dancing* (women), *finger fucking* (women), *fingering* (both), *hand job*, *flogging your log*, *frigging* (women), *jacking off*, *jerking off*, *manual manipulation* (both), *milking the monkey*, *petting your kitty* (women), *playing pocket pool*, *playing with yourself* (both), *pleasuring yourself* (both), *polishing the chrome*, *polishing the pearl* (women), *pounding your pud*, *pulling the root*, *punching the clown*, *self-love* (both), *spanking your monkey*, *stirring the cauldron* (women), *stroke job*, *taffy pulling*, *toss off*, *wank*, *whack off*, *self-love* (both), *self-service* (both), *stroking it*, *tickling your fancy* (women), *tossing off*, *yanking off*, and *yanking your crank*. The one conclusion you might draw from this list is that men spend almost as much time nicknaming their guilty pleasure as they do engaging in it. Go figure.

So there you have it. A chapter devoted to man's seemingly endless obsession to euphemize his sexual universe; a virtual thesaurus of sexually based words and phrases to help give you insight into the vernacular your man uses on those occasions when he's "shooting the shit" with his buds. Will this really help you understand your guy better? Perhaps not. But at least now you won't be tempted to frantically dial PETA or the ASPCA when you overhear a comment about simian abuse or poultry strangulation. And that's got to count for something, right?

CHAPTER FIFTEEN

What Men Hate/ What Men Like

This book has dealt mostly in generalities and this chapter is no exception. Sure tastes, likes, and dislikes vary from man to man, but there are certain things upon which men usually agree. Some you may already be familiar with, but others may take you completely by surprise. We will begin our discussion focusing on those things that are repugnant to most men. Knowing what these are allows you to either live harmoniously with your significant other or torture him mercilessly. Choose whichever option you like.

The following is a list of people, places, and things that men detest (in no particular order of heinousness):

1. Granny panties

2. Linen stores

3. White sales

4. Going dancing at a club (after marriage—particularly true of white, American men)

5. Waiting for you to do "one more thing" before sex

6. Excuses to *not* have sex

7. Being unfavorably compared to your father, your brother, your brother-in-law, his brother, your ex, your high-school sweetheart, his boss, the guy who took your virginity, or any other male who's seen you naked

8. Nagging*

9. You uttering the words, "We need to talk."

10. Sharing our feelings

11. Losing our hair

12. Flannel nighties (yours, not ours)

13. The phrase "You should know why I'm upset"

14. "Helpful" suggestions on how we might improve ourselves

15. "Cozies"

16. Hearing you state, "I hate to say I told you so ..." (which you obviously don't hate to say nearly as much as we hate to *hear* you say it—because we see it merely as gloating wrapped in a blanket of ingenuous sensitivity)

17. Hairspray and the accompanying noxious fumes

18. Anyone betting us on something, losing, then refusing to pay up

19. Your soliciting our opinion then disregarding it

20. A swift kick in the crotch

* *Nagging* deserves special elaboration. Nothing is less appreciated by guys than the incessant reiteration of the same point or desire (with the possible exception of, "fuck me, fuck

me, fuck me!"). And we're equally annoyed by it regardless of the source. We hate it from our kids, our parents, our teachers, our preachers, and our significant others. And when combined with its two ugly partners-in-crime, *whining* and *complaining*, it is enough to make us want to bite off our own ears so we don't have to listen to it anymore ... or at the very least, spend as little time as possible with the perpetrator of this destructive verbal assault. Few things are less productive and more injurious to a relationship in the long run than nagging. If you must employ this as a persuasive technique (and I strongly discourage this), do so sparingly. Your relationship will be better for it.

Now to the things that most of us with a Y chromosome cherish. While making us happy has traditionally been summarized by the Three Fs (*F*eed us, *F*latter us, and *F*uck us"), a more expansive list should prove to be substantially more enlightening. Herewith are the things that make us want to get out of bed each day:

1. Sex

2. Gadgets

3. Good food (although specific cuisine preferences vary from man to man)

4. Logic (as long as it can't be used against us)

5. Reading on the toilet (our idea of "multitasking")

6. Technology

7. Being able to successfully provide financially for ourselves and our families

8. Sex

9. Competition (athletic or otherwise)

10. Catherine Zeta Jones (naked or otherwise)

11. Breasts (most organic varieties and some hybrids)

12. Sandwiches (a subset of item #3, but worth a special mention)

13. The idea of owning a boat (the reality of actually owning a boat is far less satisfying)

14. Swiss army knives

15. Sex

16. Praise (doesn't have to be sincere, we just have to believe it)

17. Dirty limericks (we just love rhyming with "Nantucket")

18. Any odor produced by our own body

Of course, there are always exceptions to the preceding list. And what some men adore, others abhor. But in general, most of the things on the "hate list" or "like list" are likely to be true for most of the straight men you meet, work with, or see naked. And if our lists seem to lack emotional and spiritual complexity, oh well. It's just who we are. But don't despair in that. Rejoice! Our relative simplicity makes us fairly easy to understand ... and please. Armed with this knowledge, you are well on your way to fully understanding what makes your man (or anyone else's, for that matter) tick. By avoiding the items on the first list and embracing those on the second you now hold the key to fostering harmony and good will in your relationship ... and basically getting any guy to do anything you want them to *and* thank you for it afterwards. See, buying this book was a really wise investment. Tell all your friends.

CHAPTER SIXTEEN

Men: A Review

So there you have it: The male mind in all its glorious beauty and simplicity. If you've paid careful attention, the previously inscrutable thought process of men is now not quite so difficult to understand. And for those of you who were skimming, speed-reading, multitasking, or operating a motor vehicle while absorbing this book's contents, I am providing you with a brief bullet-point summary:

- Men and women think differently.

- Men and women have a different language. Men can usually be taken quite literally. "Fine" means fine, "yes" means yes and "I don't care" means I don't care. There is rarely hidden meaning or layers of subtext in our communication. If you want to know "what we meant by that," you will get your answer from simply taking whatever we said at face value.

- Sex is very important to men. We are drawn to women who will have regular sex with us, while those who won't will quickly lose their appeal.

- Money is also important to men, primarily because financial security is appealing to women. We know that the more wealth we acquire, the more women we attract. And the more women we attract, the greater opportunity for possible sexual encounters. In a nut-shell—we get paid so we can get laid. Vulgar, but true.

- Men will say just about anything to get you to sleep with them.

- Men aren't really sure whether they like you or not until after you consummate your relationship.

- Men like women that look like women. We like boobs, buns, bushy or bare beavers, preferably unwrapped and pressed against us.

- We don't care about fashion or trendy hairstyles.

- We are uninterested in how much money you have or make.

- Respecting you is not important to our loving or desiring you.

- Men cheat because they are given the opportunity. Cheating does not, however, necessarily indicate any displeasure or dissatisfaction with our relationship with *you*.

- Men don't change simply because you want them to. If you're looking for a fixer-upper, invest in real estate.

- Men masturbate because they need the release. They start as soon as they discover this magical ability and continue until rigor mortis sets in or their penis wears out ... whichever comes first.

- The only non-business-related reason a straight man asks you out is because he wants inside your pants.

- Subtlety is lost on most men. When you communicate with guys, be explicit about what you want or need.

- Men get their self-worth from their accomplishments, not from their relationships.

- Men are generally happy with who they are and not interested in self-help books or unsolicited advice on how they might improve.

- Men aren't insensitive. We simply keep our feelings to ourselves. And we're perfectly okay with that. You might as well be, too.

- Other than sex, men look to their significant others mostly for support. Men gravitate to women who make them feel good about themselves and retreat from those who don't.

- Men don't care about the minutiae. We're more into the big picture. We care that you wrecked the car. We care *not* that the other driver smelled like Juniper Breeze and carried a Louis Vuitton purse that must have been a knock-off, because she was driving a Kia and her nails were obviously press-ons. If you listen carefully you can almost hear our eyes glaze over.

- Men are big proponents of the "if it ain't broke, don't fix it" school of thought. On our own, we're unlikely to want to rearrange the furniture, get a new hairstyle, or change the rules of a relationship.

- Your unattached, straight male friends would sleep with you if invited to do so (assuming you're not repulsive, psychotic, or plagued with open sores or a contagious, incurable disease).

- And, of course … every man sees you naked.

I do hope you enjoyed our little journey and that your new-found knowledge translates into more effective communication, better understanding, and improved interaction with all the men in your life. And if your sex life improves … that wouldn't be so bad either. At least then your guy won't be so annoyed with me for "spilling the beans" on the secrets of the male mind. And if he's basking in the afterglow of more plentiful, greatly improved sexual encounters, he might just overlook my "loose lips" and be tempted to send me a thank you note. Just remember to tell him to direct that note to the editorial offices of *Cosmopolitan* (with whom I have no affiliation). That you heard all this "man stuff" from me has to remain our little secret. Thanks for your discretion and good luck in all your encounters with those strange, sheet-stealing creatures that inhabit the bed beside you.

Lightning Source UK Ltd.
Milton Keynes UK
13 April 2010

152713UK00001B/139/P